The New Generation of
MANGA ARTISTS
THE Kao Yung & Kuan-Liang PORTFOLIO   Vol. 5

THE NEW GENERATAION OF MANGA ARTISTS
VOL. 5: The Kao Yung & Kuan-Liang Portfolio

Copyright © 2004 Kao Yung, Kuan-Liang
Copyright © 2004 Graphic-sha Publishing Co., Ltd.

This book was first designed and published in Japan in 2004 by Graphic-sha Publishing Co., Ltd.
This English edition was published in 2004 by Graphic-sha Publishing Co., Ltd.
Sansou Kudan Bldg. 4th Floor, 1-14-17 Kudan-kita, Chiyoda-ku, Tokyo 102-0073 Japan
Tel: +81-(0)3-3263-4318 Fax: +81-(0)3-3263-4318

Original Cover and Text Page Design:	Shinichi Ishioka
English translation management:	Língua fránca, Inc. (an3y-skmt@asahi-net.or.jp)
Editor:	Kuniyoshi Masujima (Graphic-sha Publishing Co., Ltd.)
Editorial collaborator:	Michiharu Nishihashi
Foreign Language edn. Project Coordinator:	Kumiko Sakamoto (Graphic-sha Publishing Co., Ltd.)

First printing: February 2004

ISBN: 4-7661-1438-8
Printed and bound in China by Everbest Printing Co., Ltd.

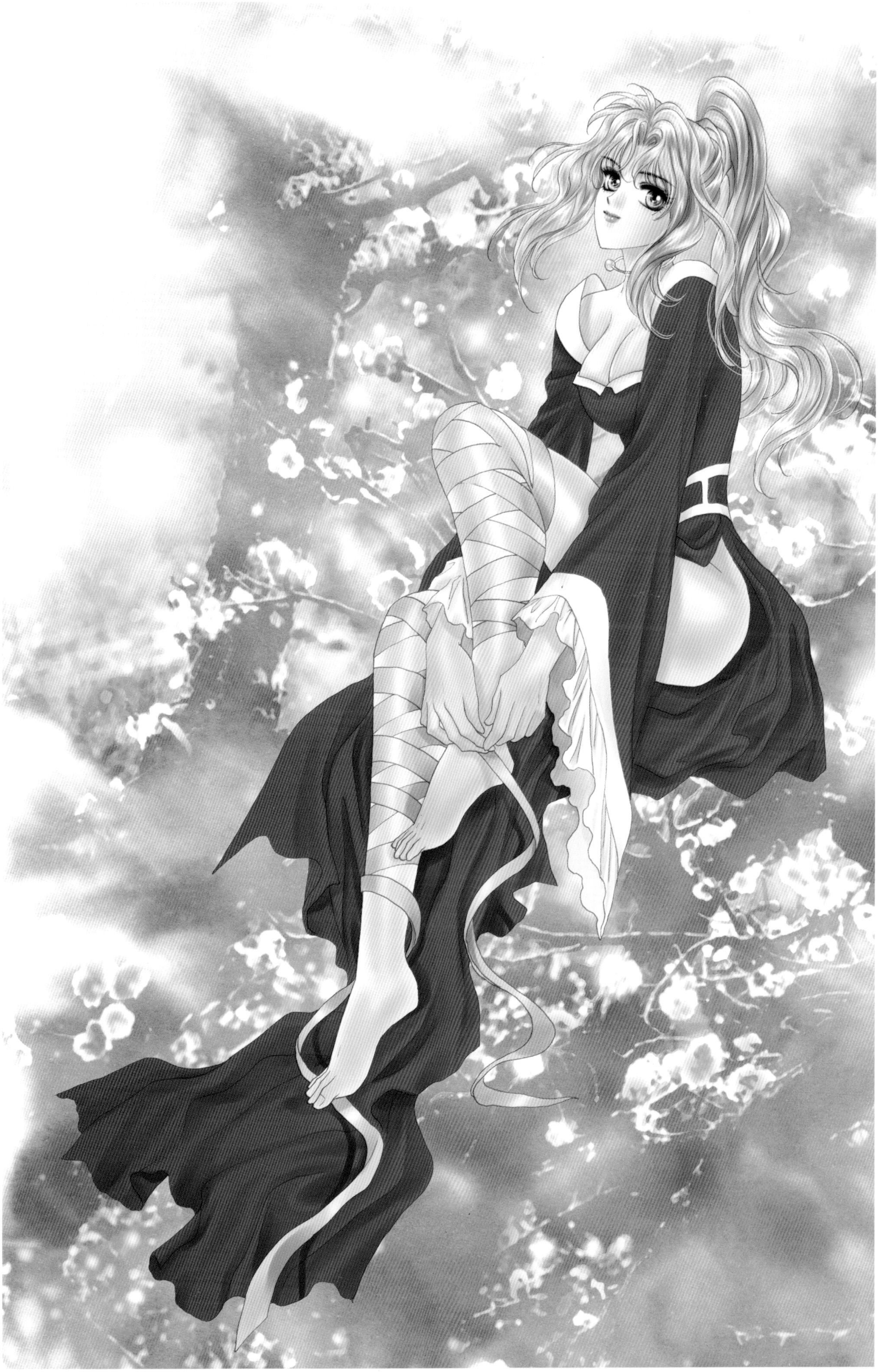

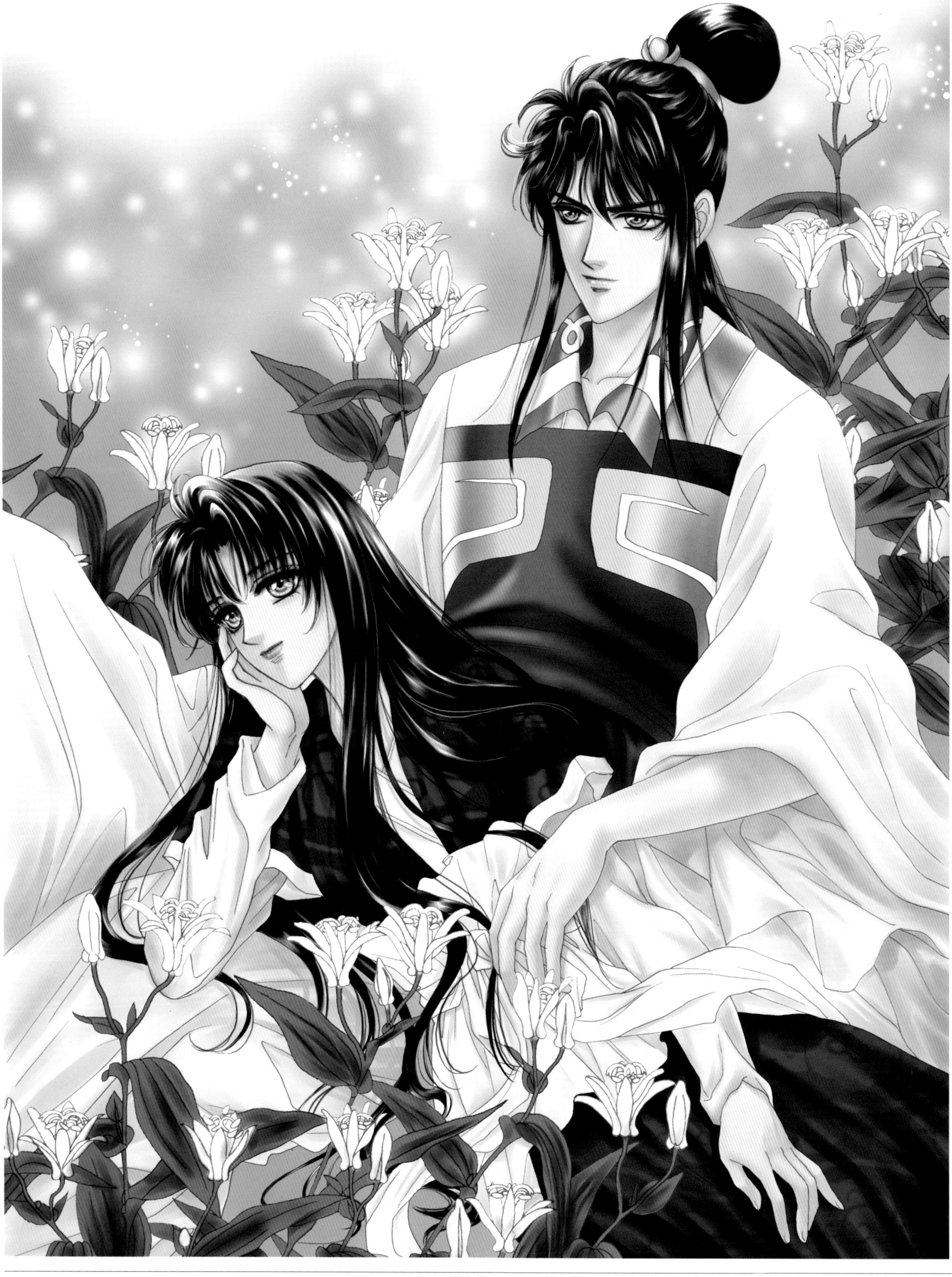

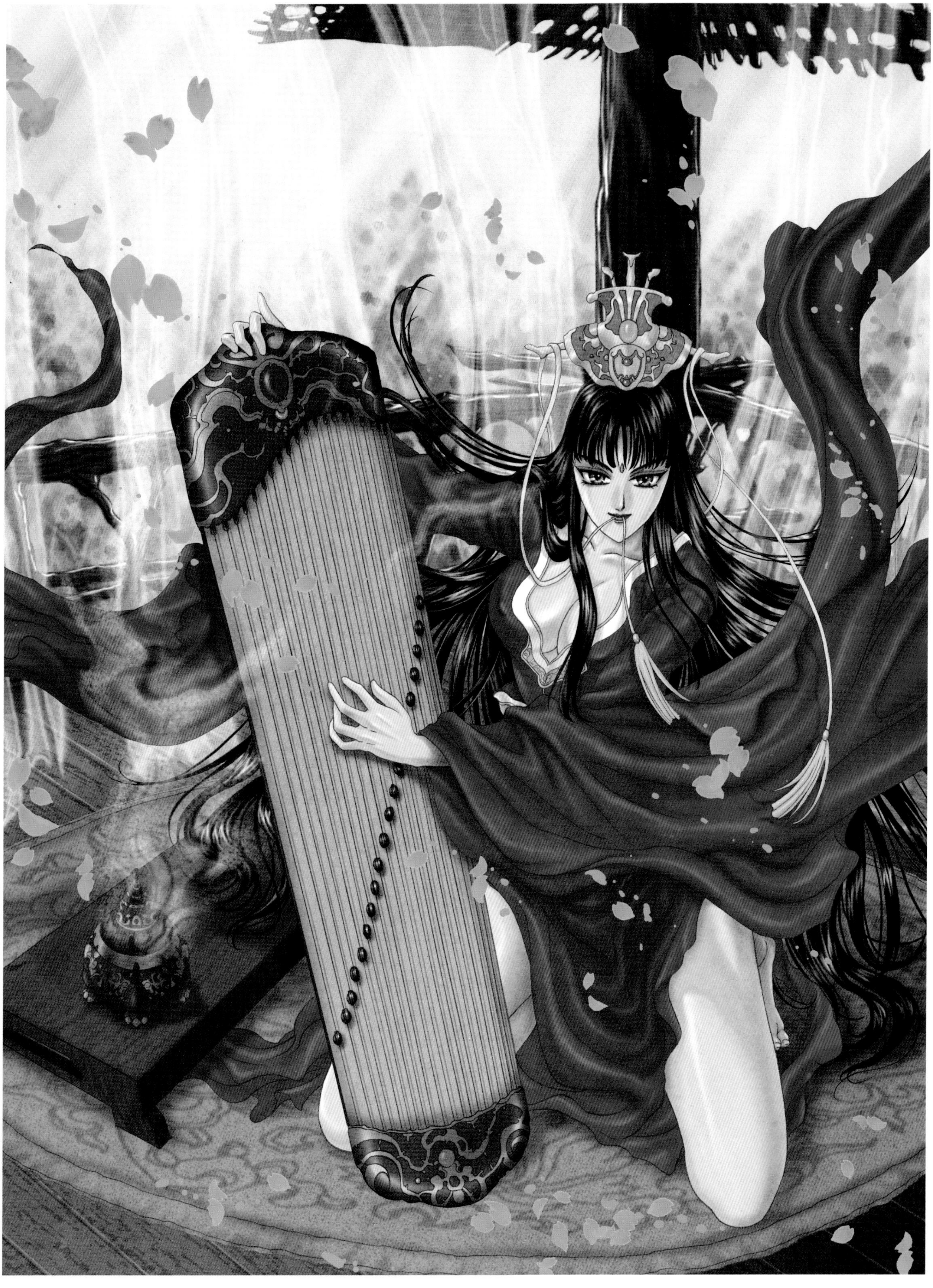

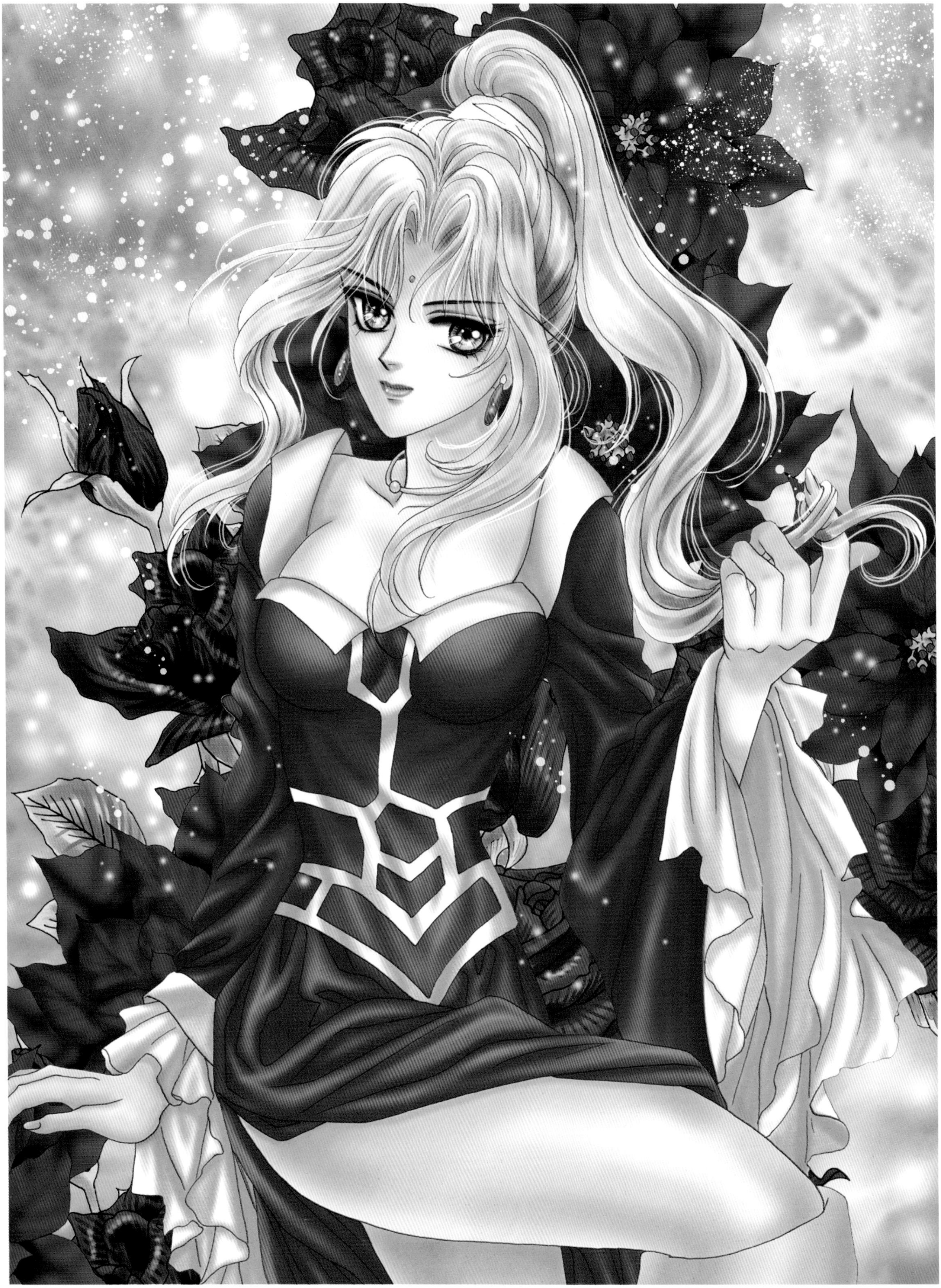

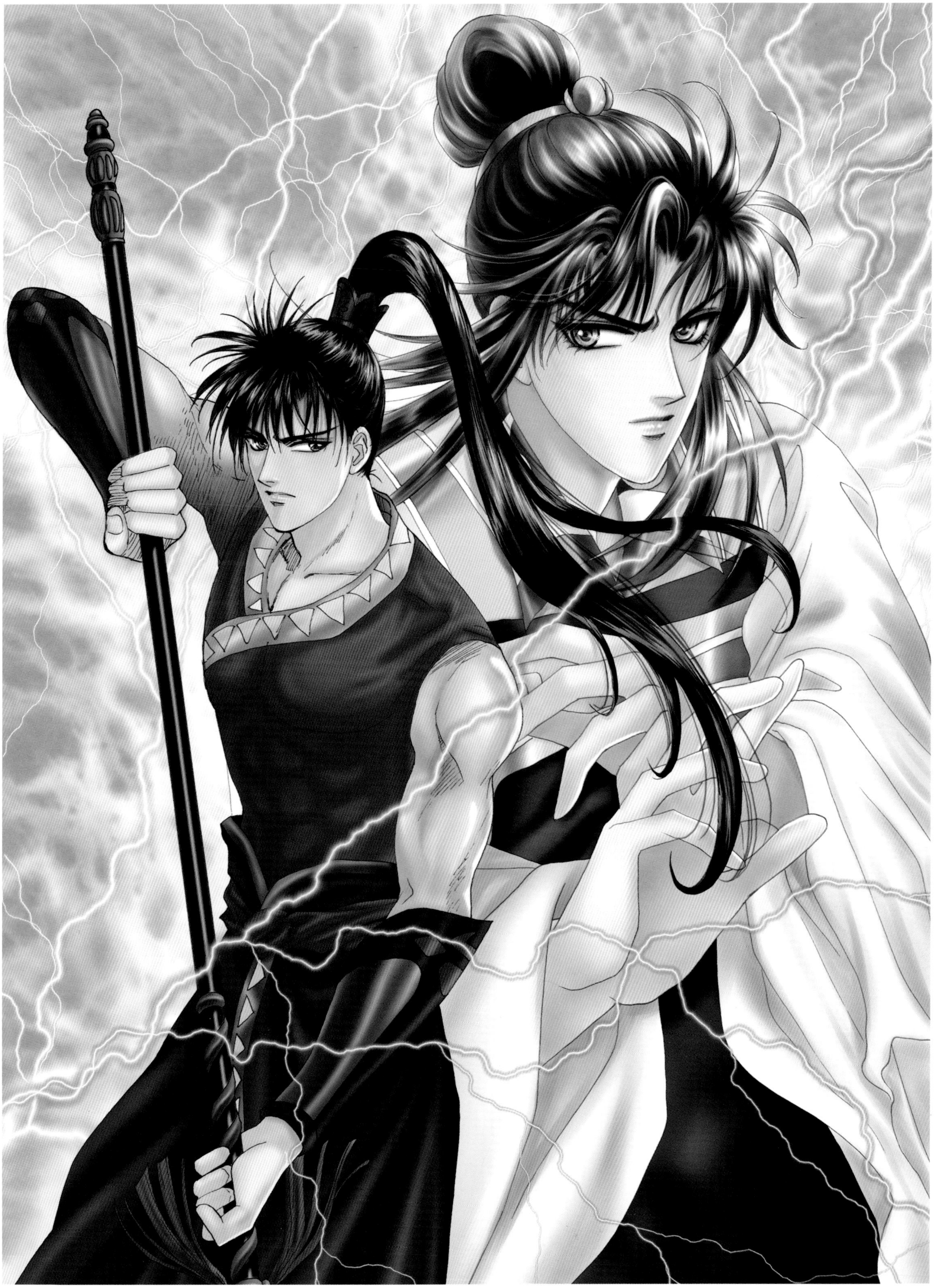

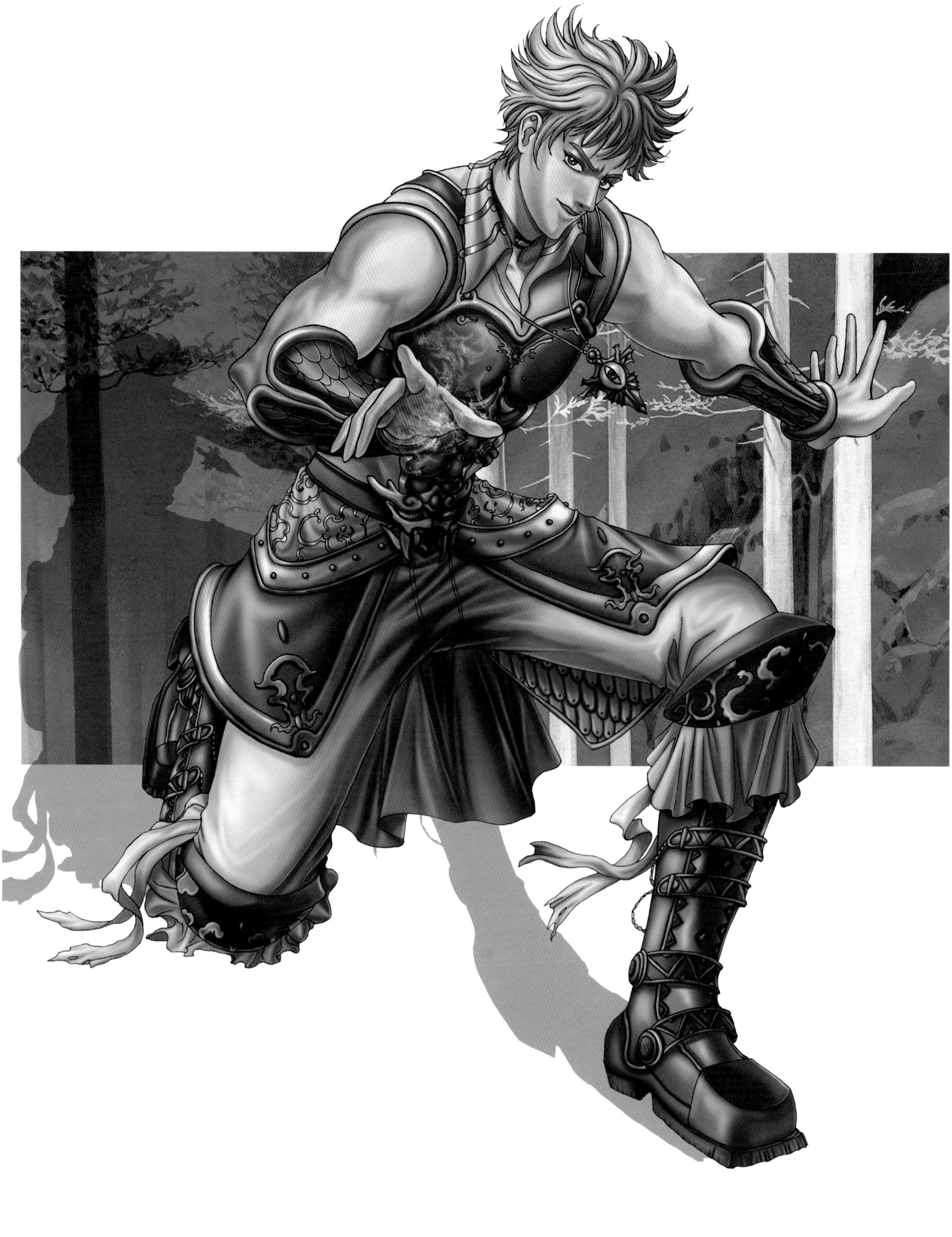

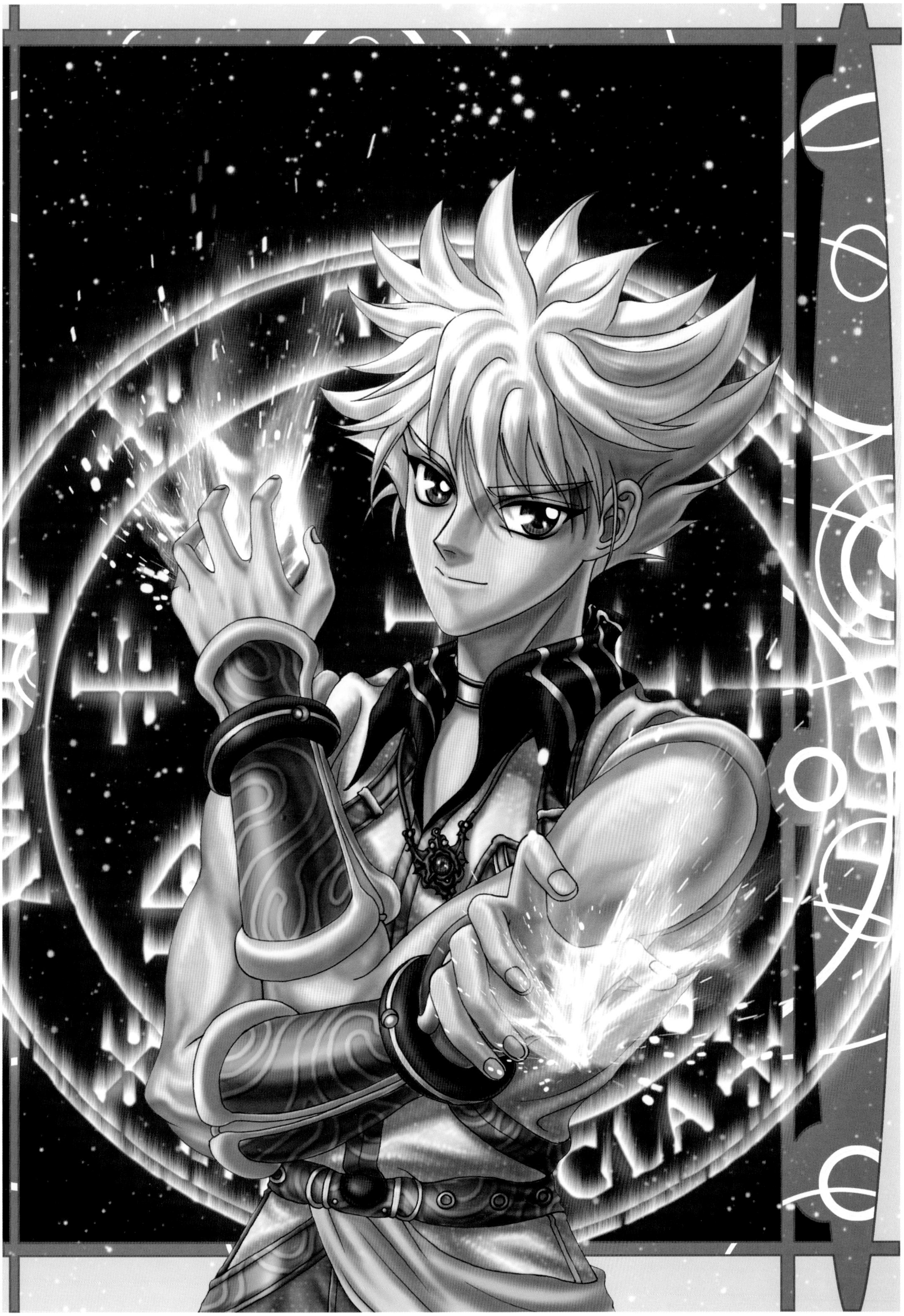

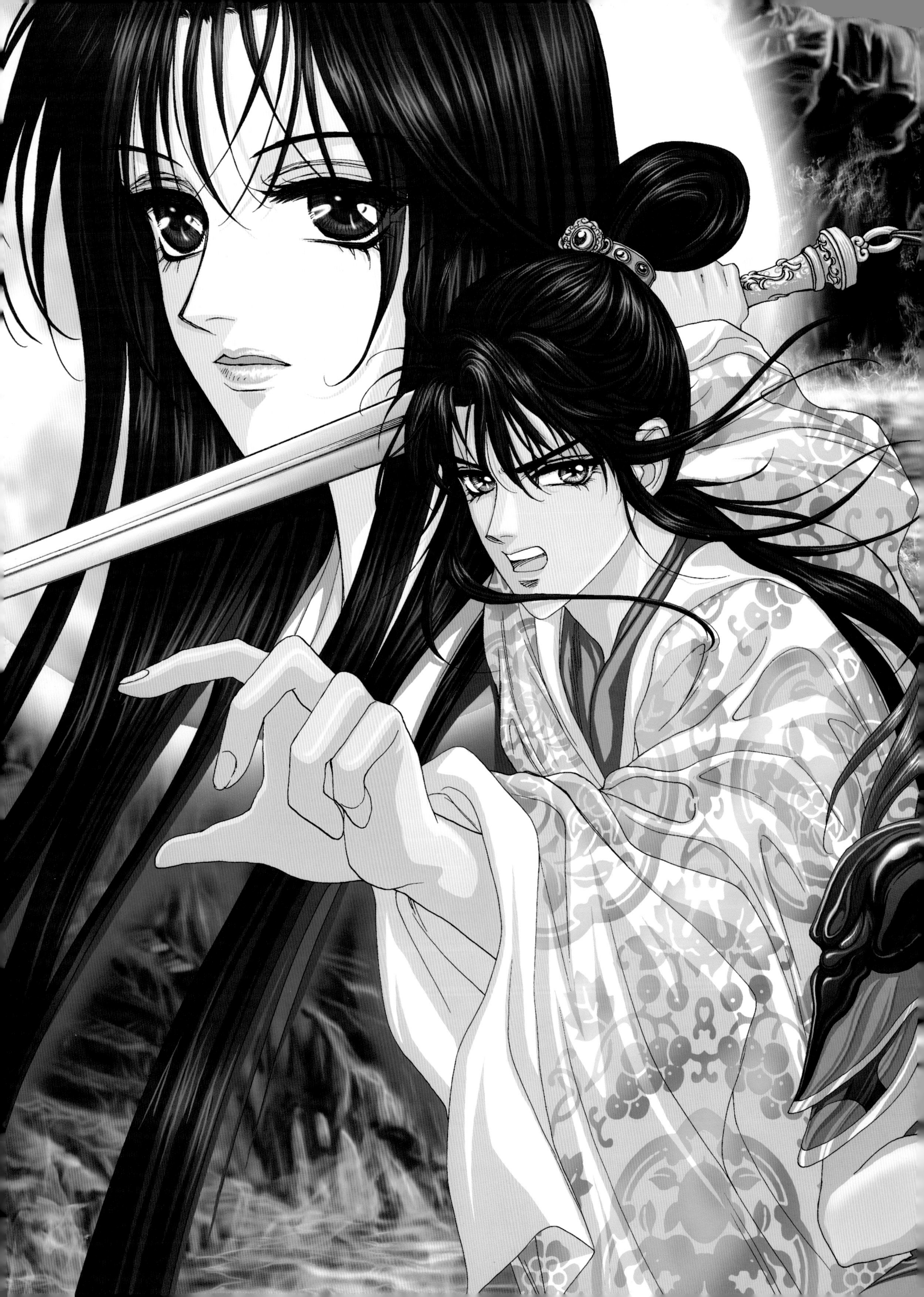

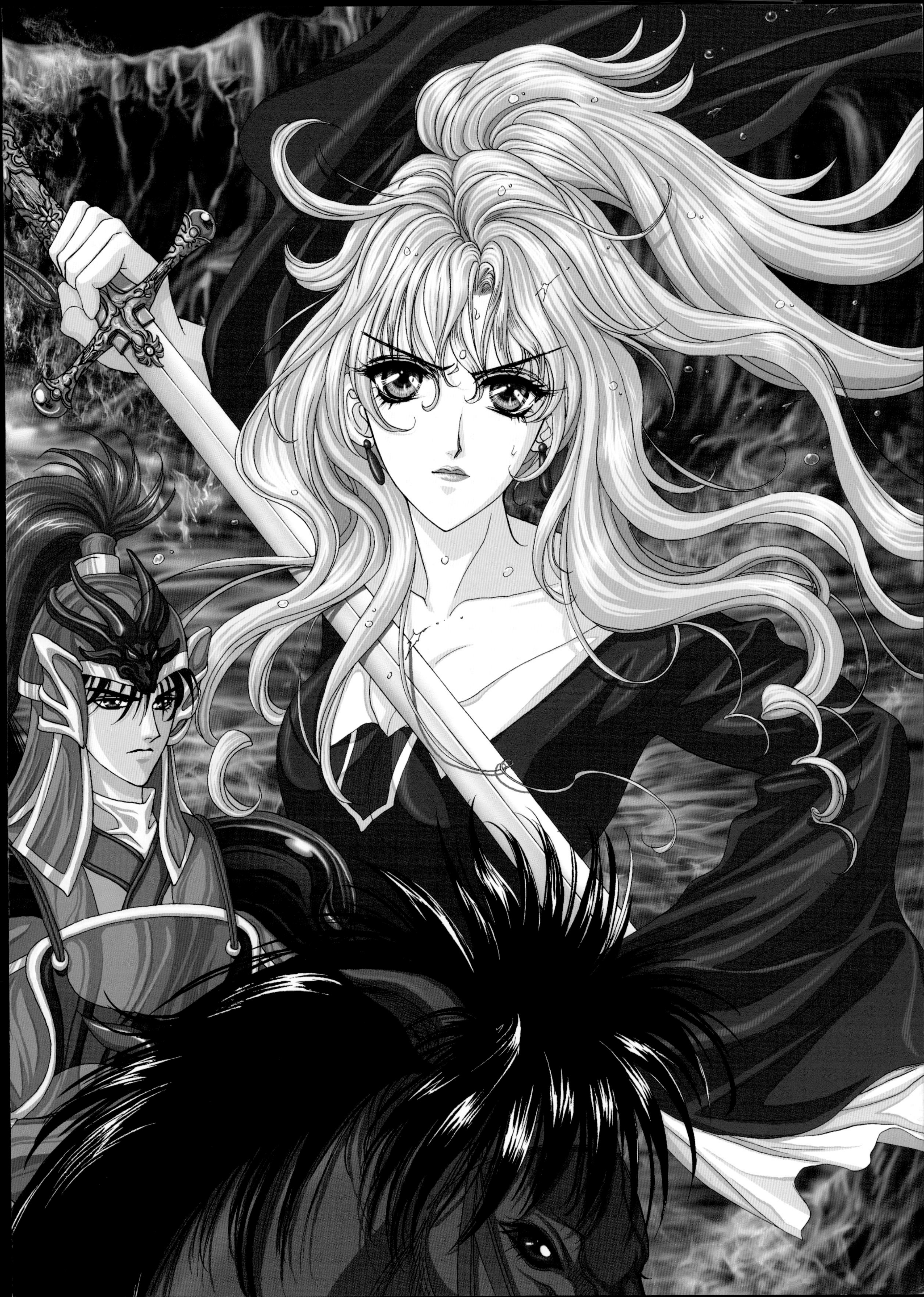

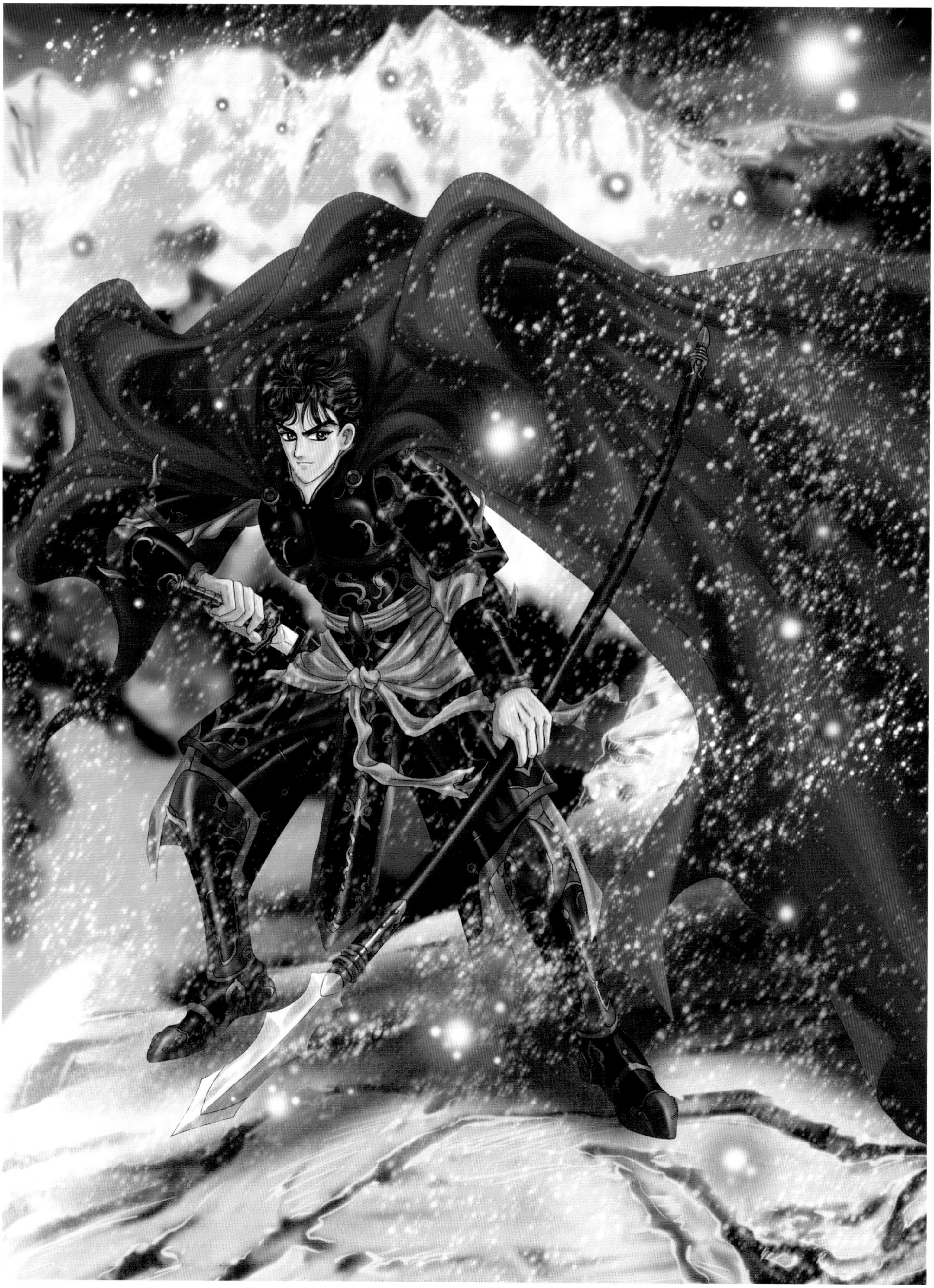

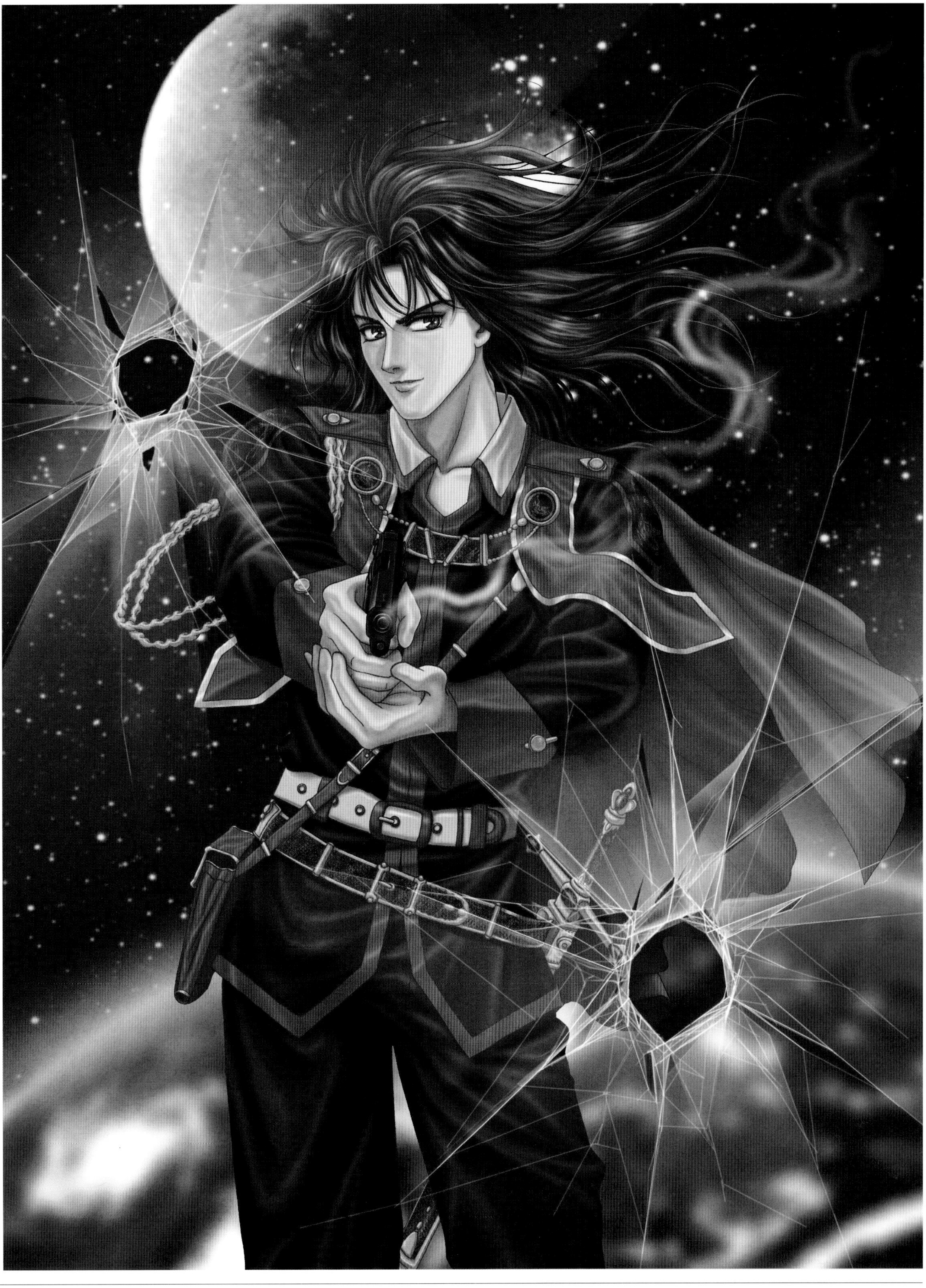

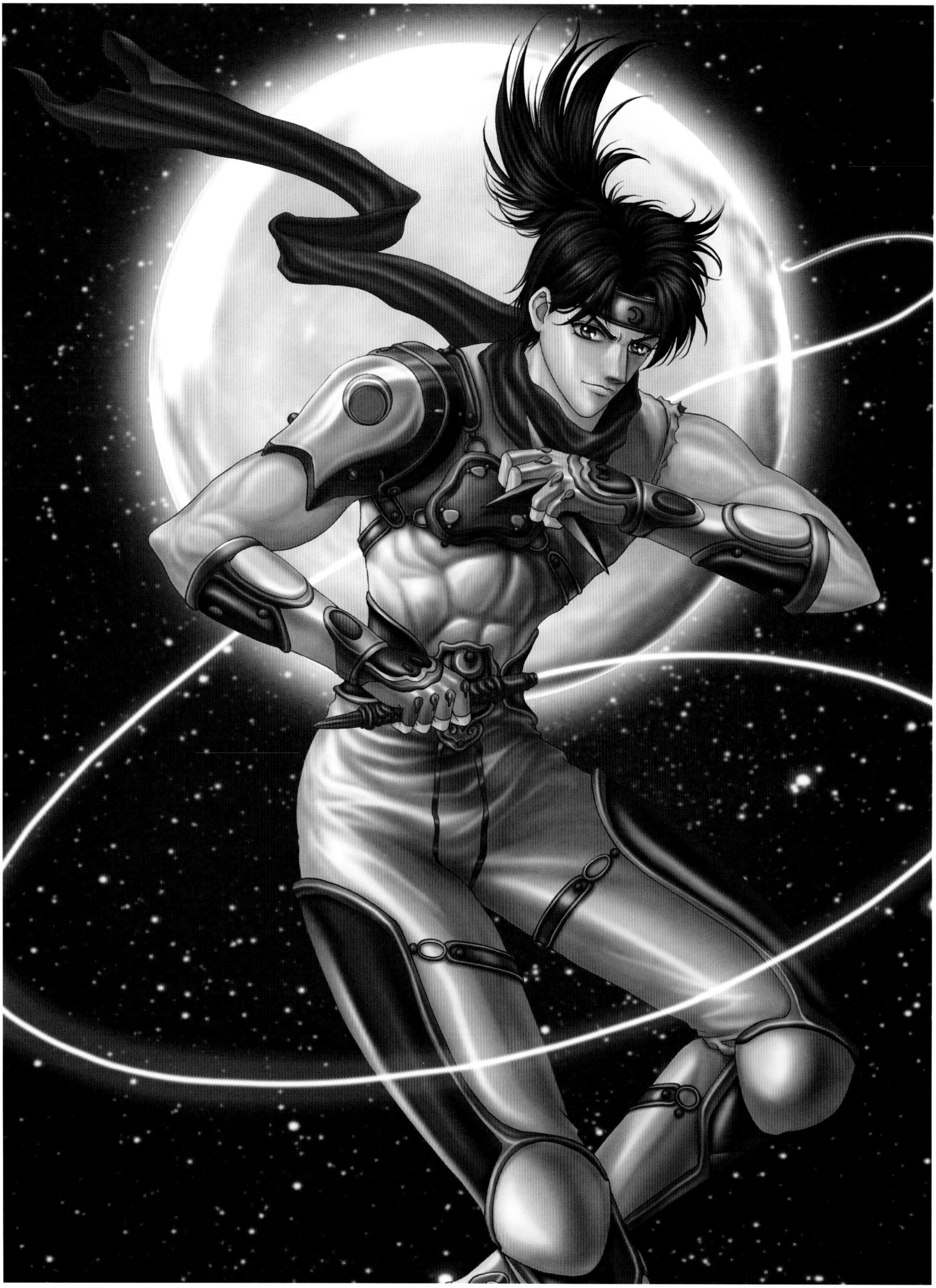

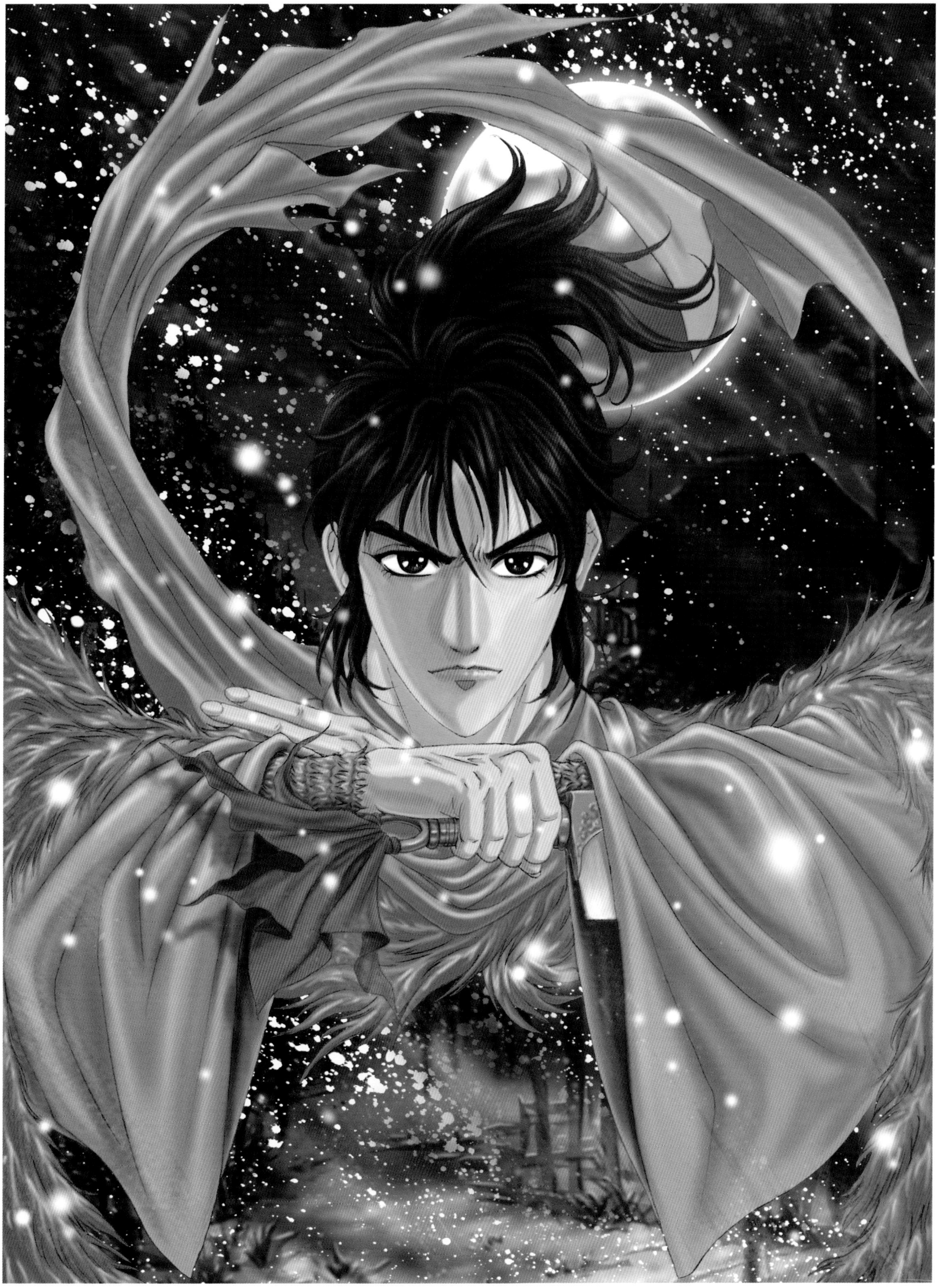

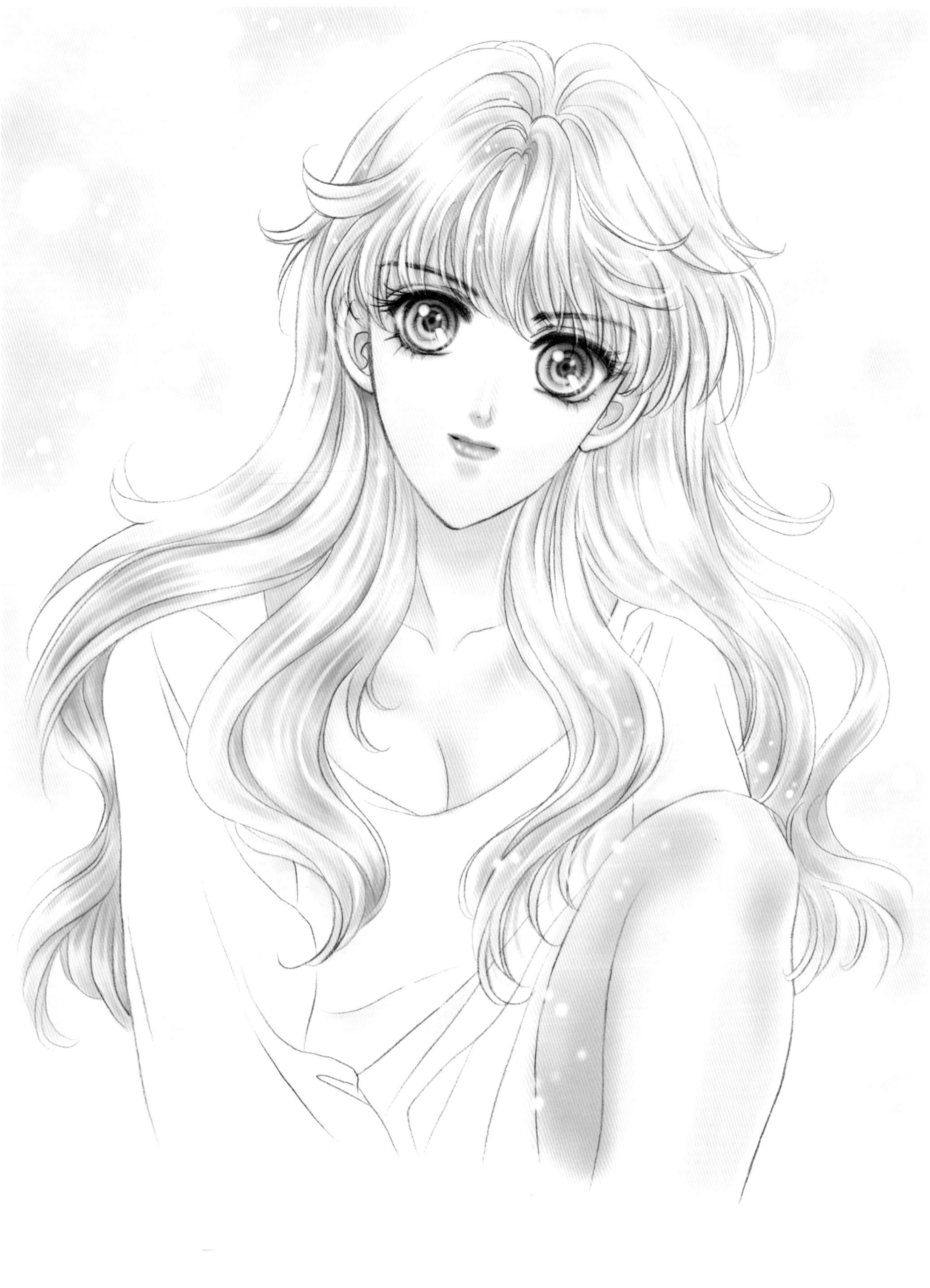

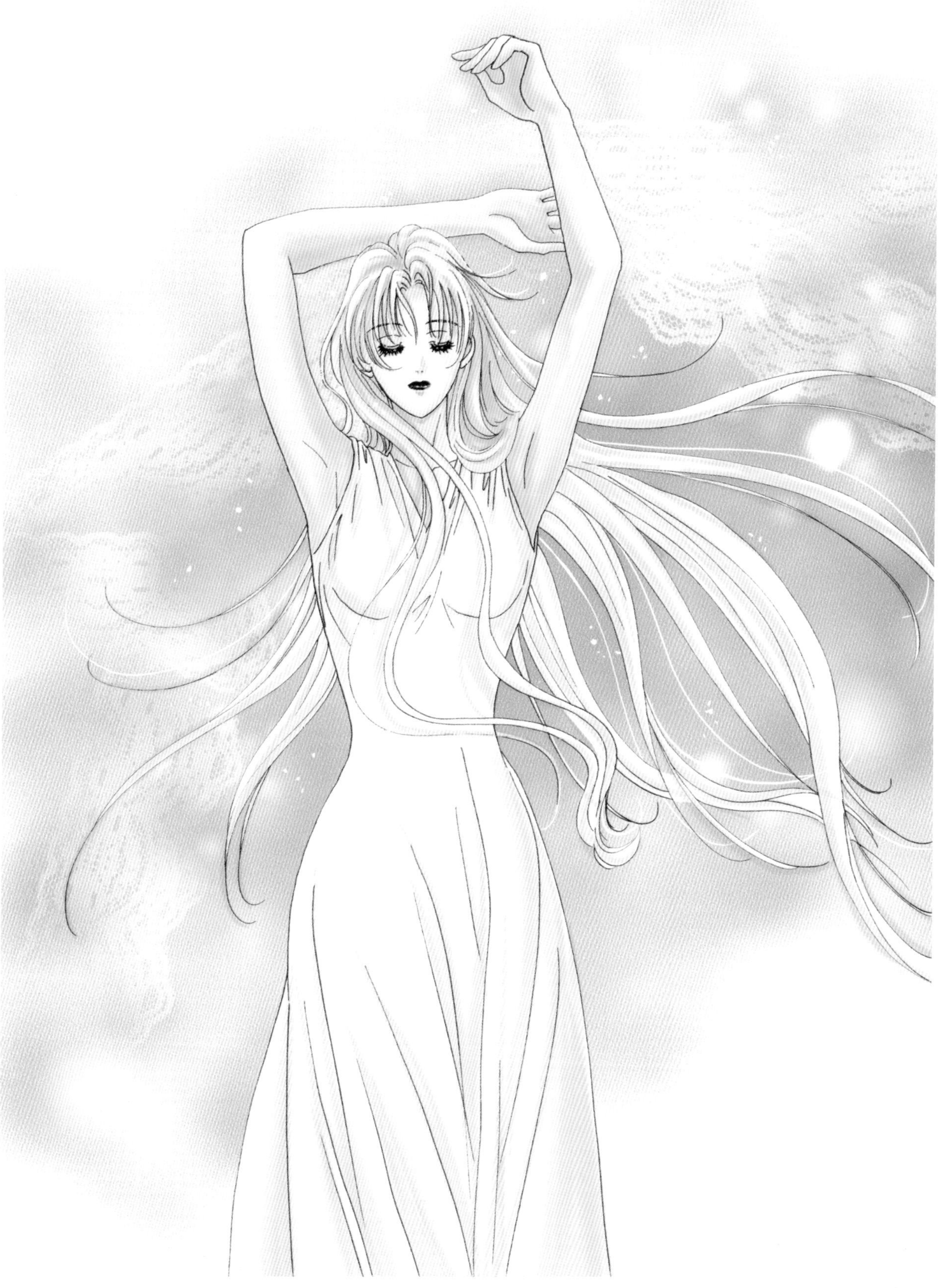

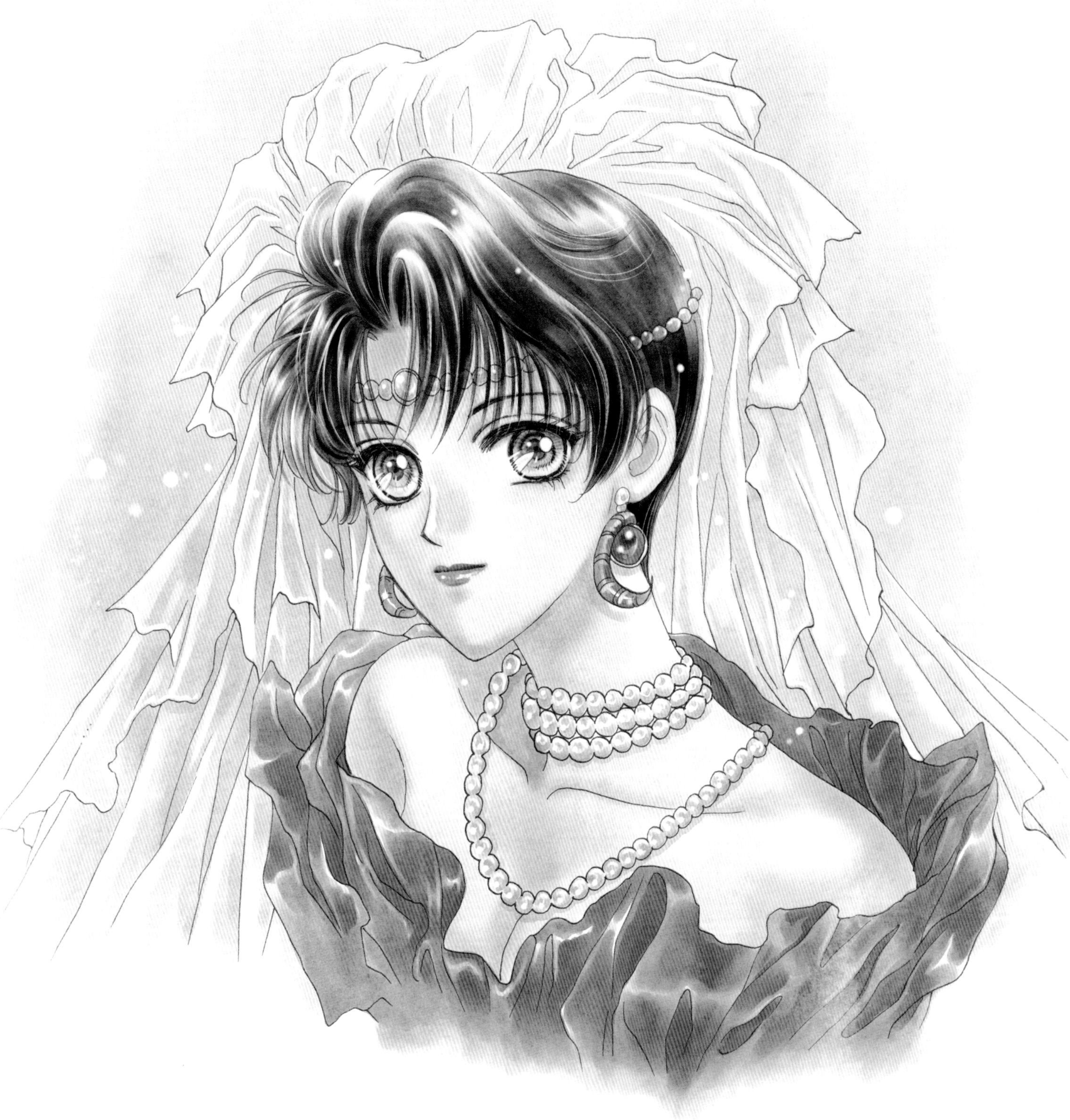

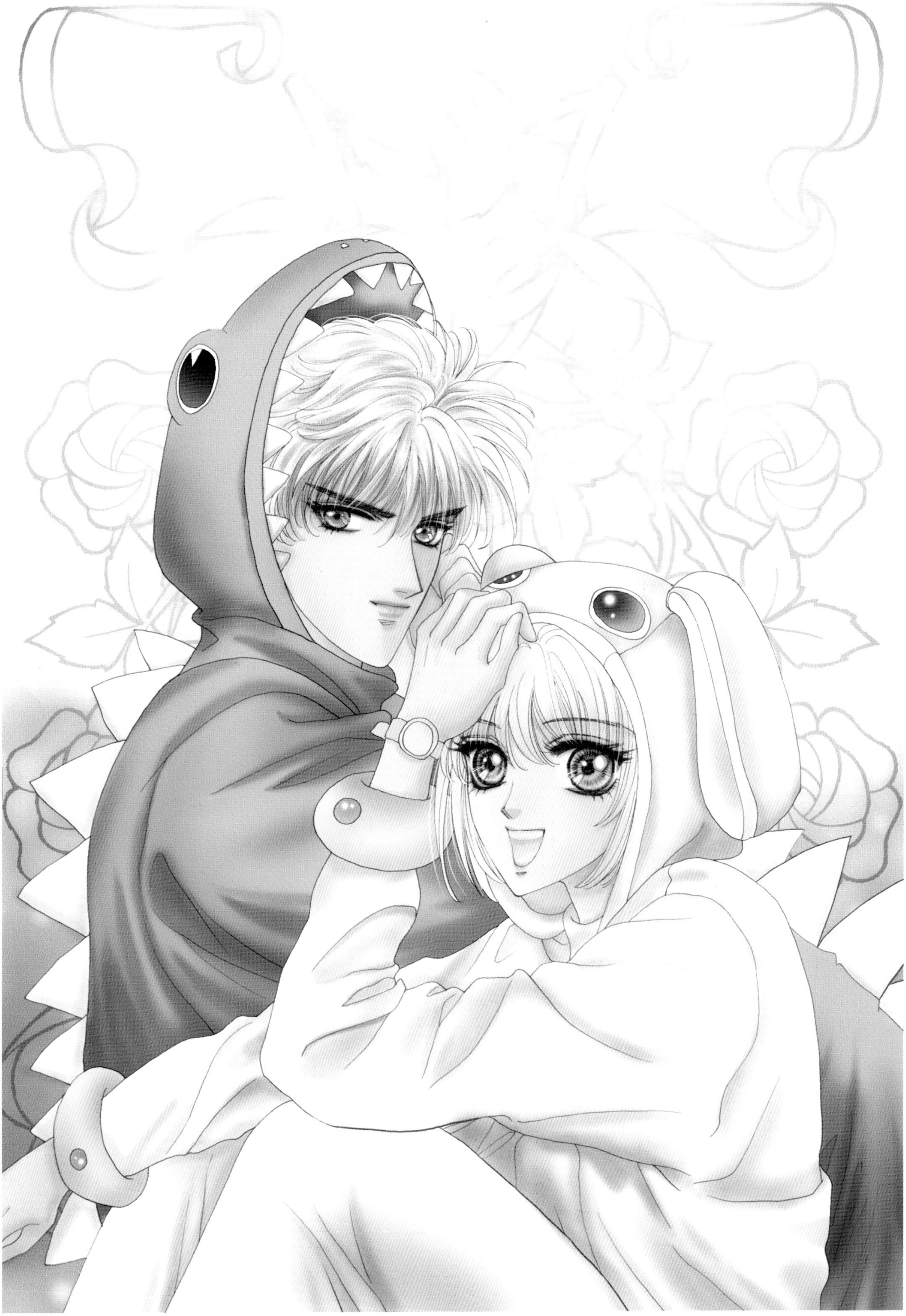

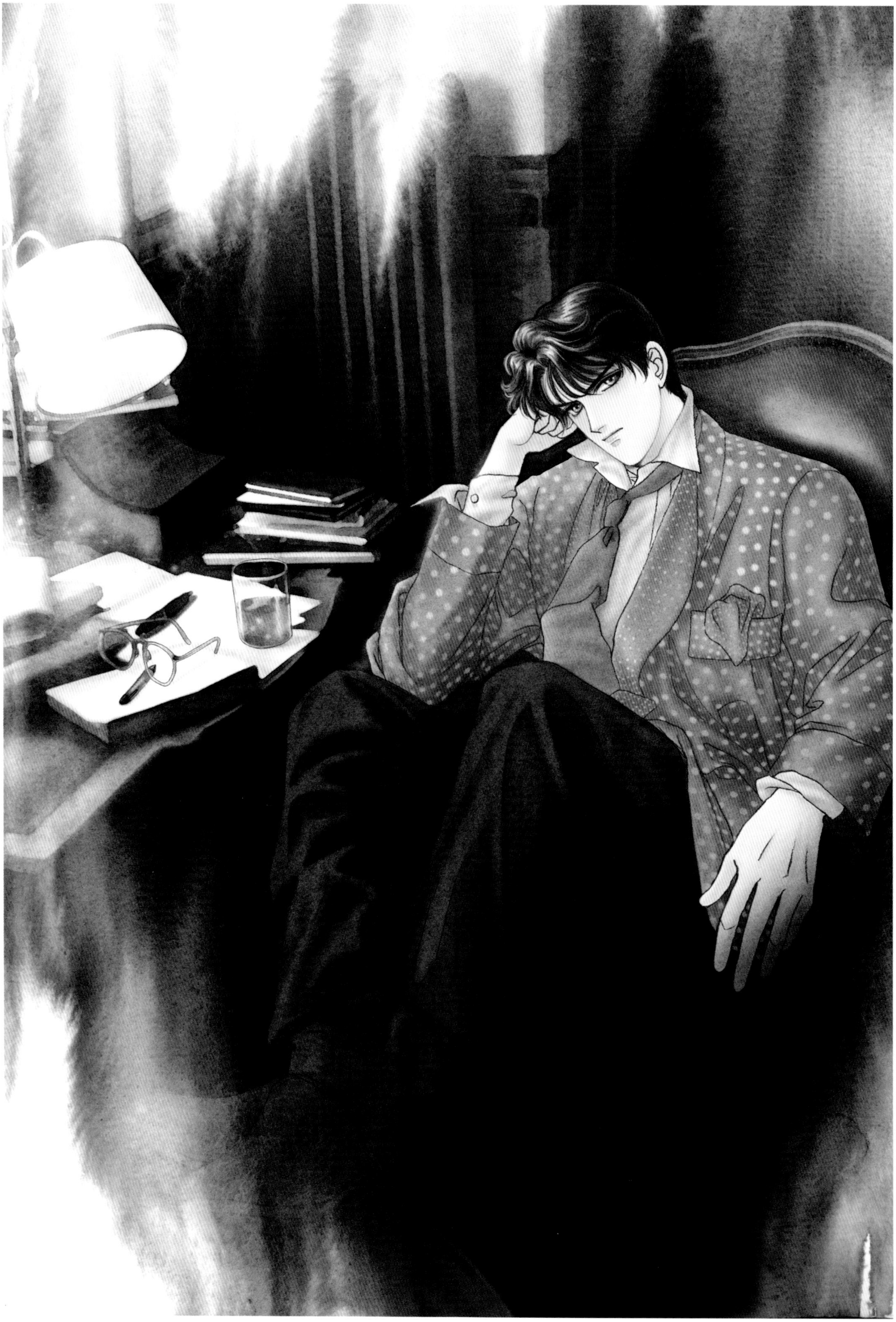

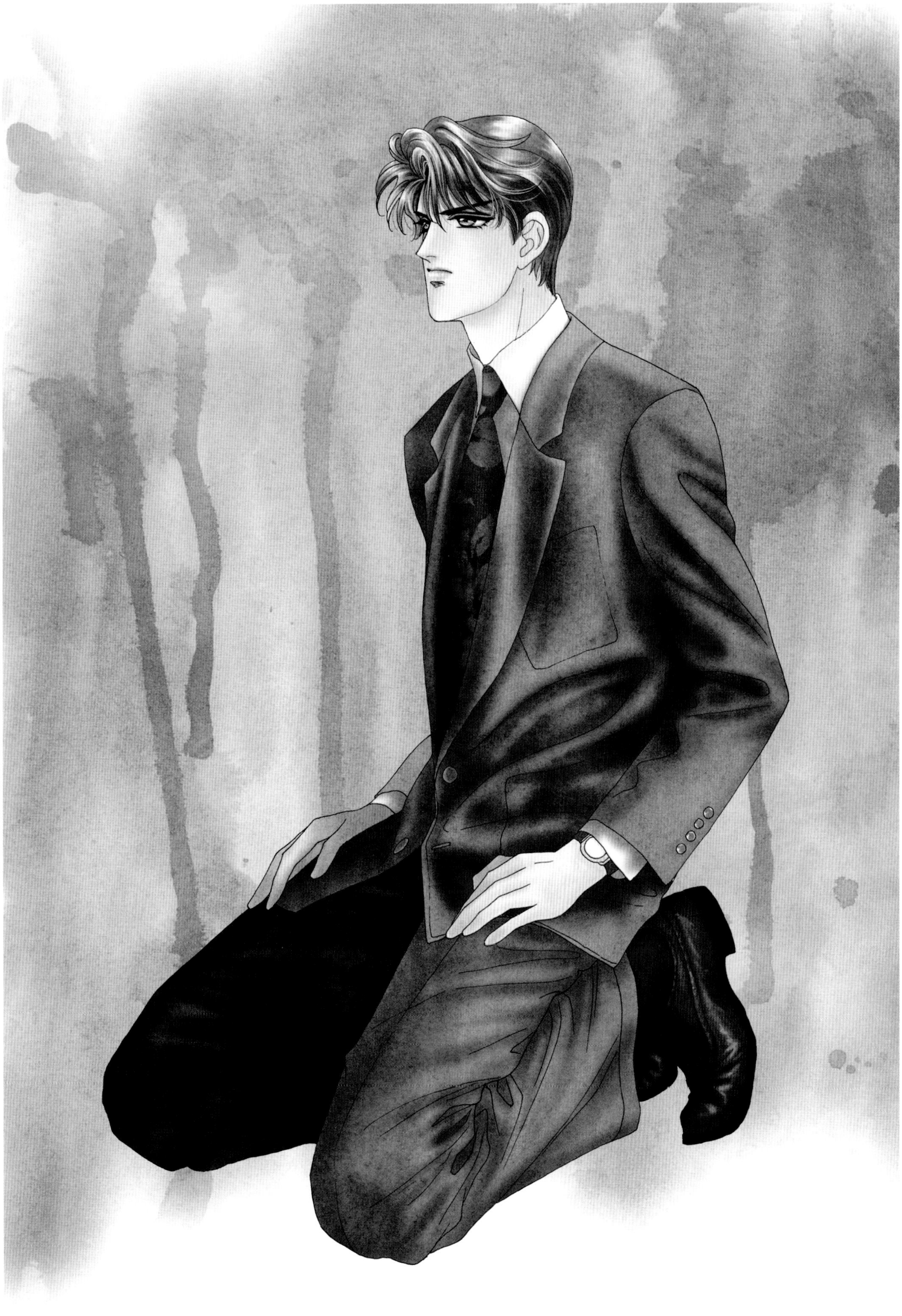

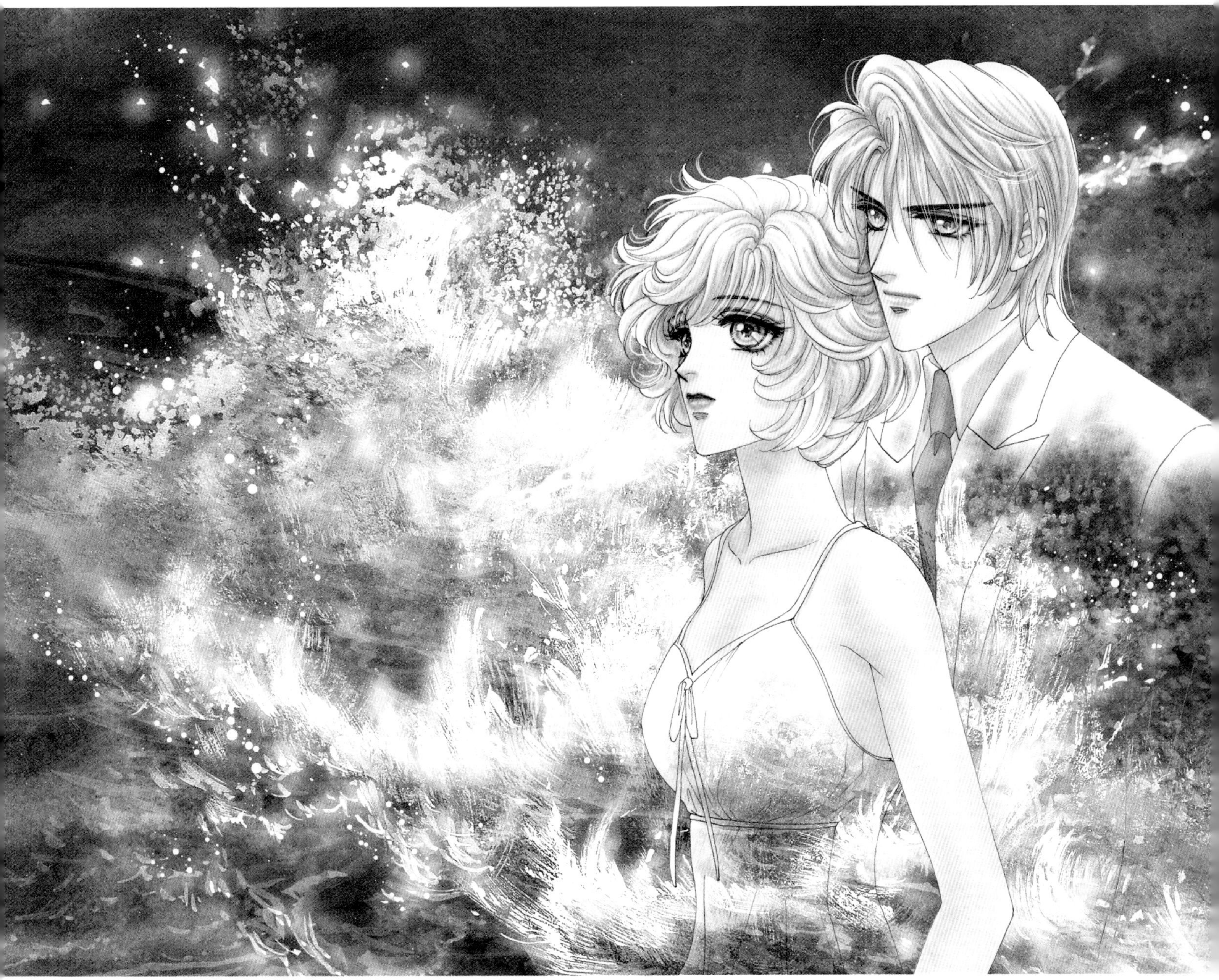

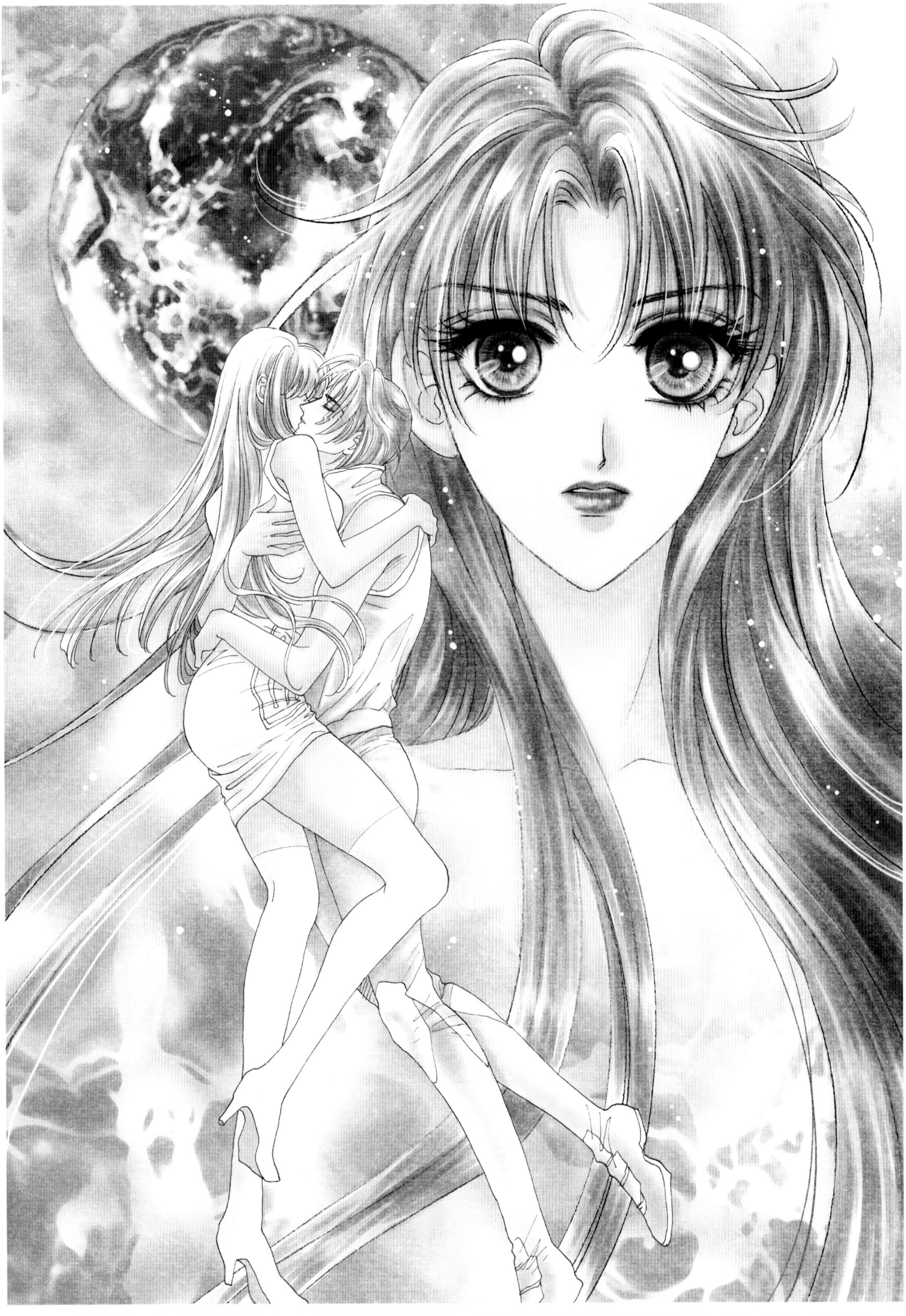

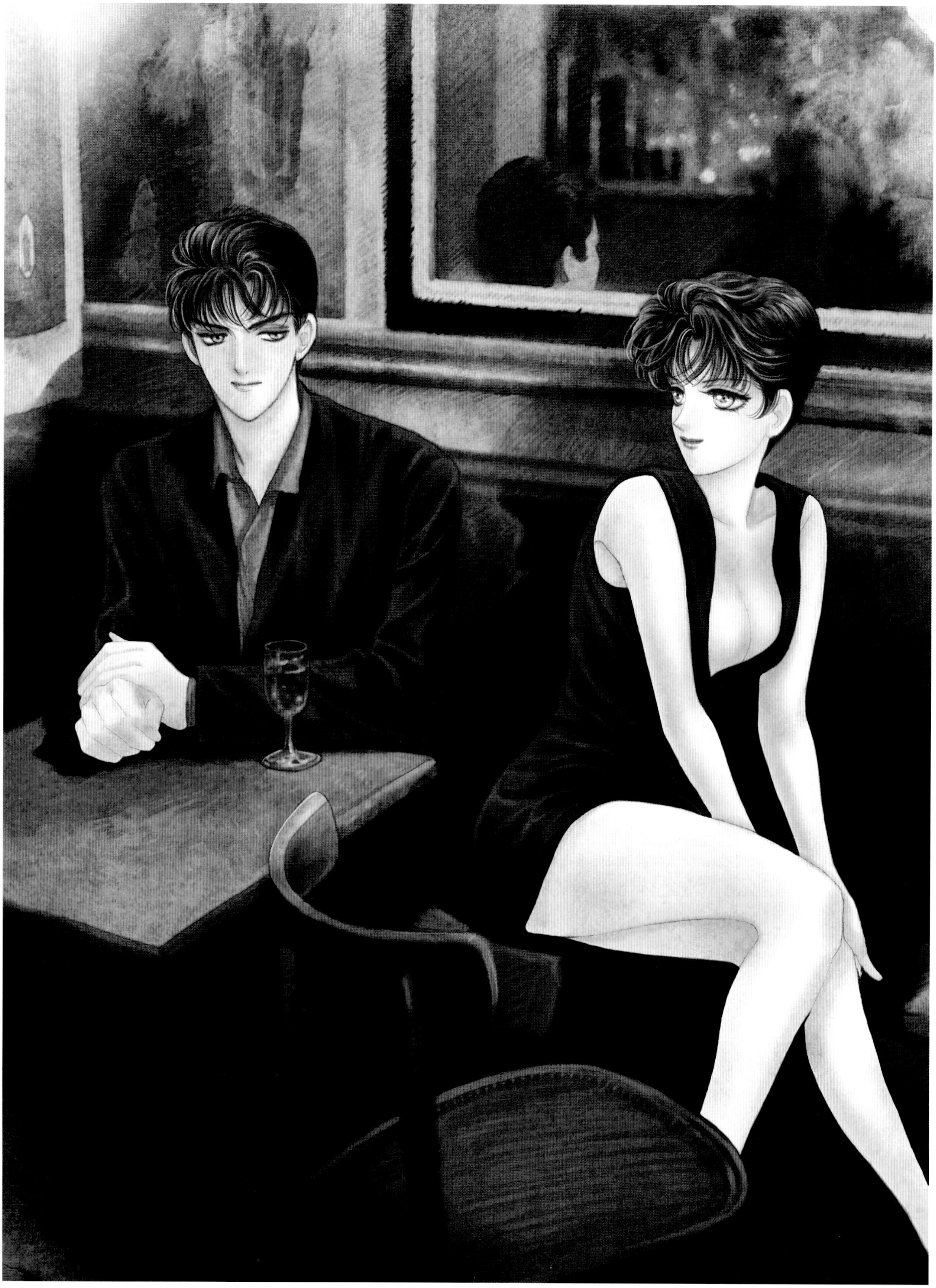

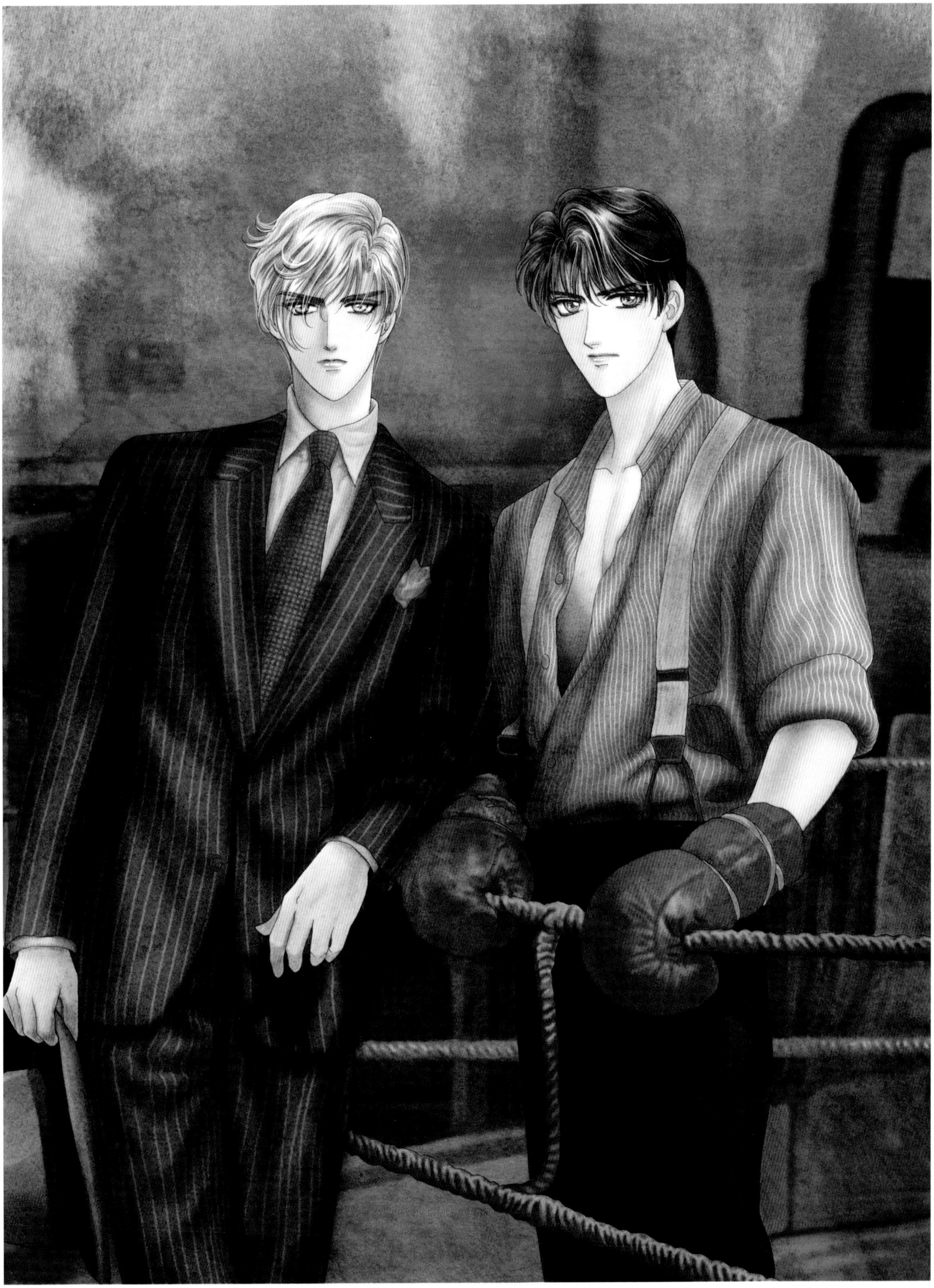

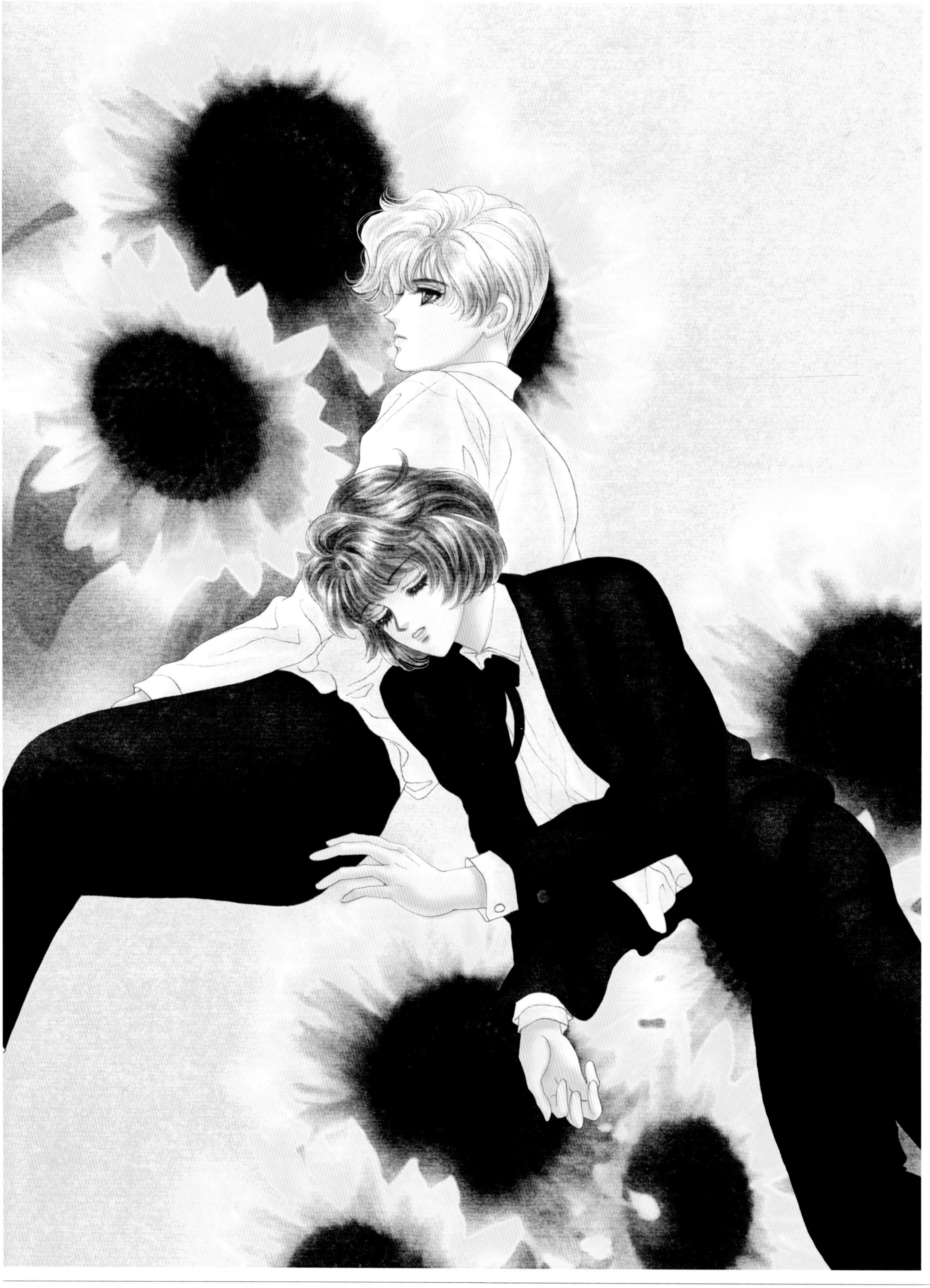

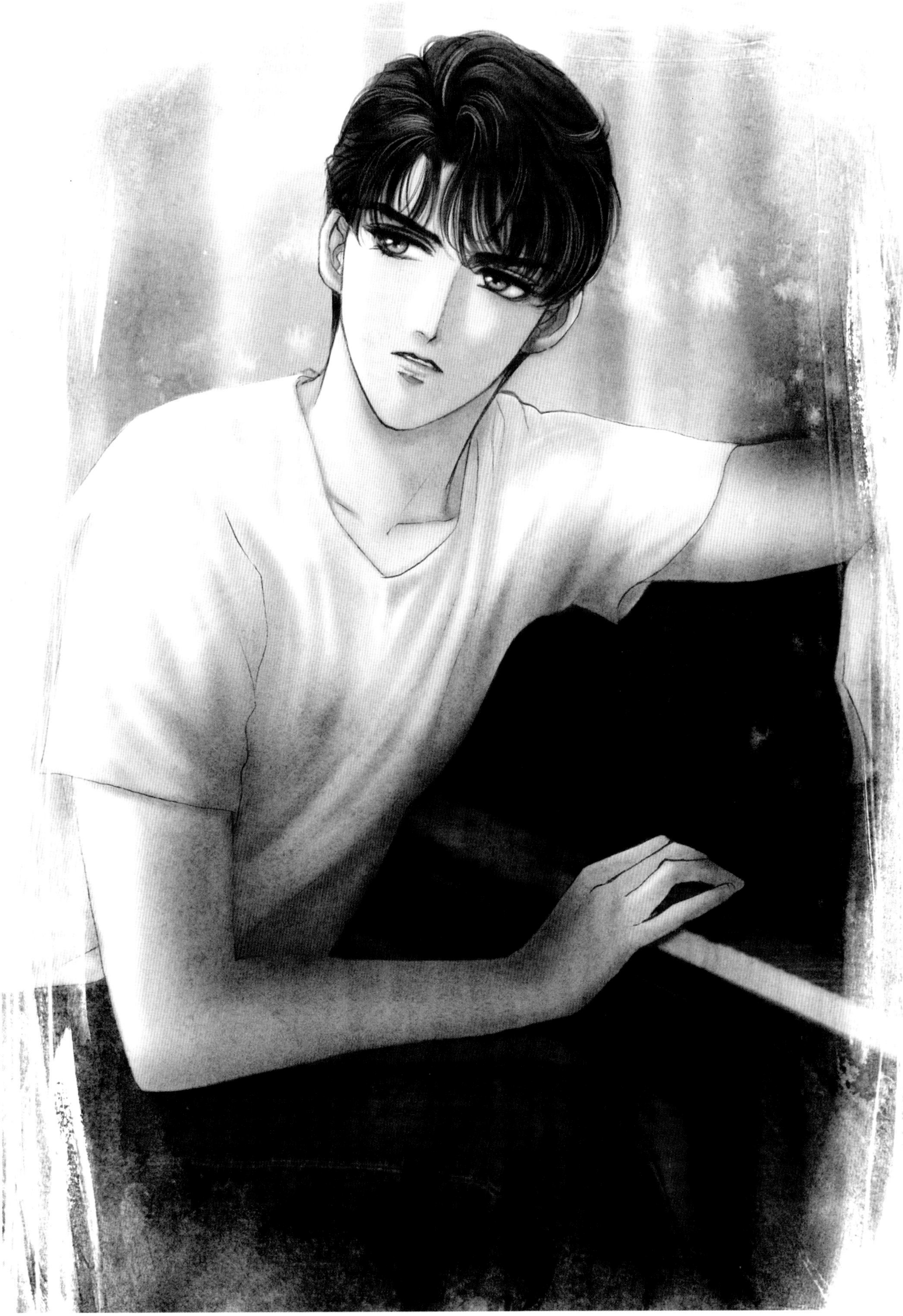

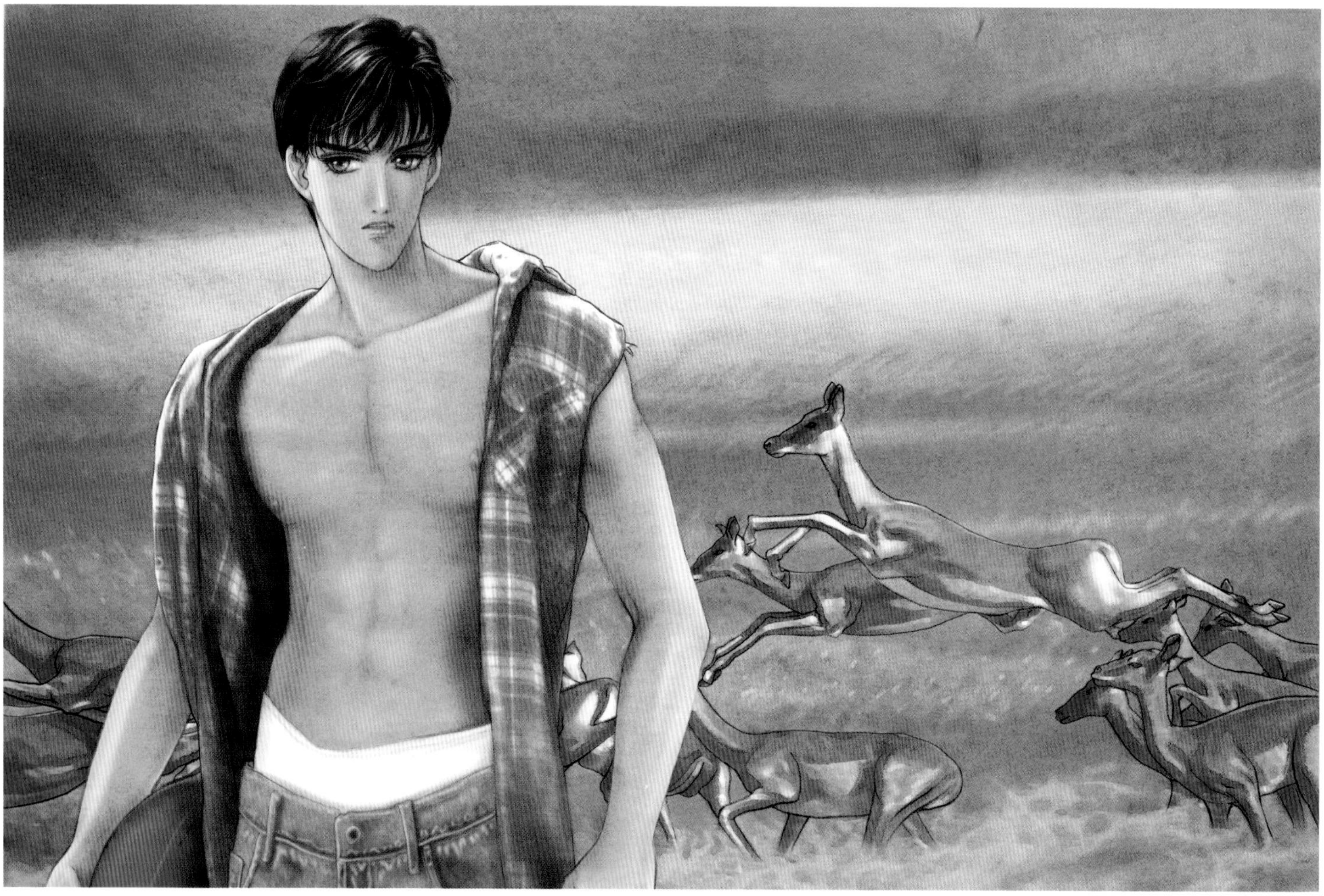

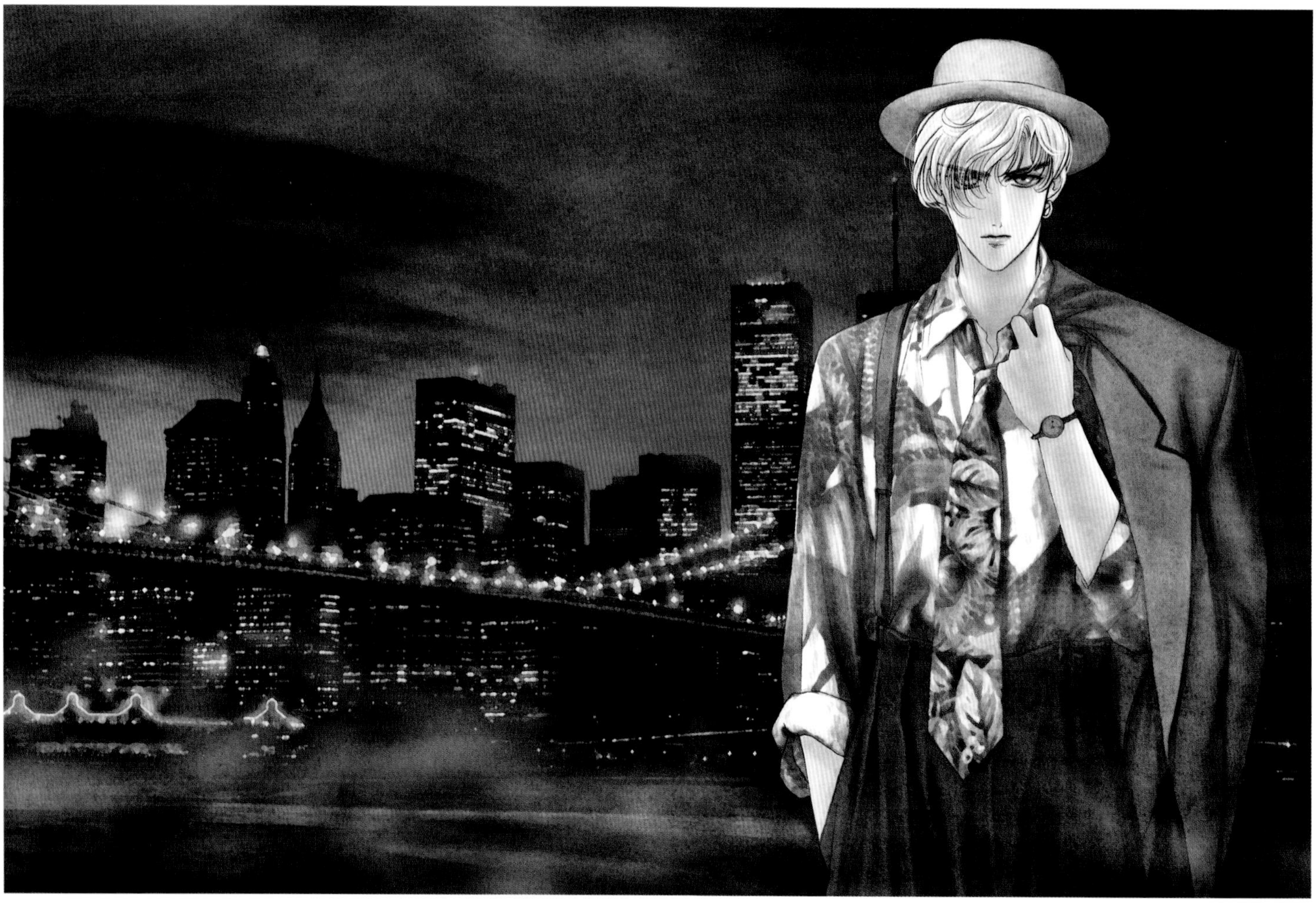

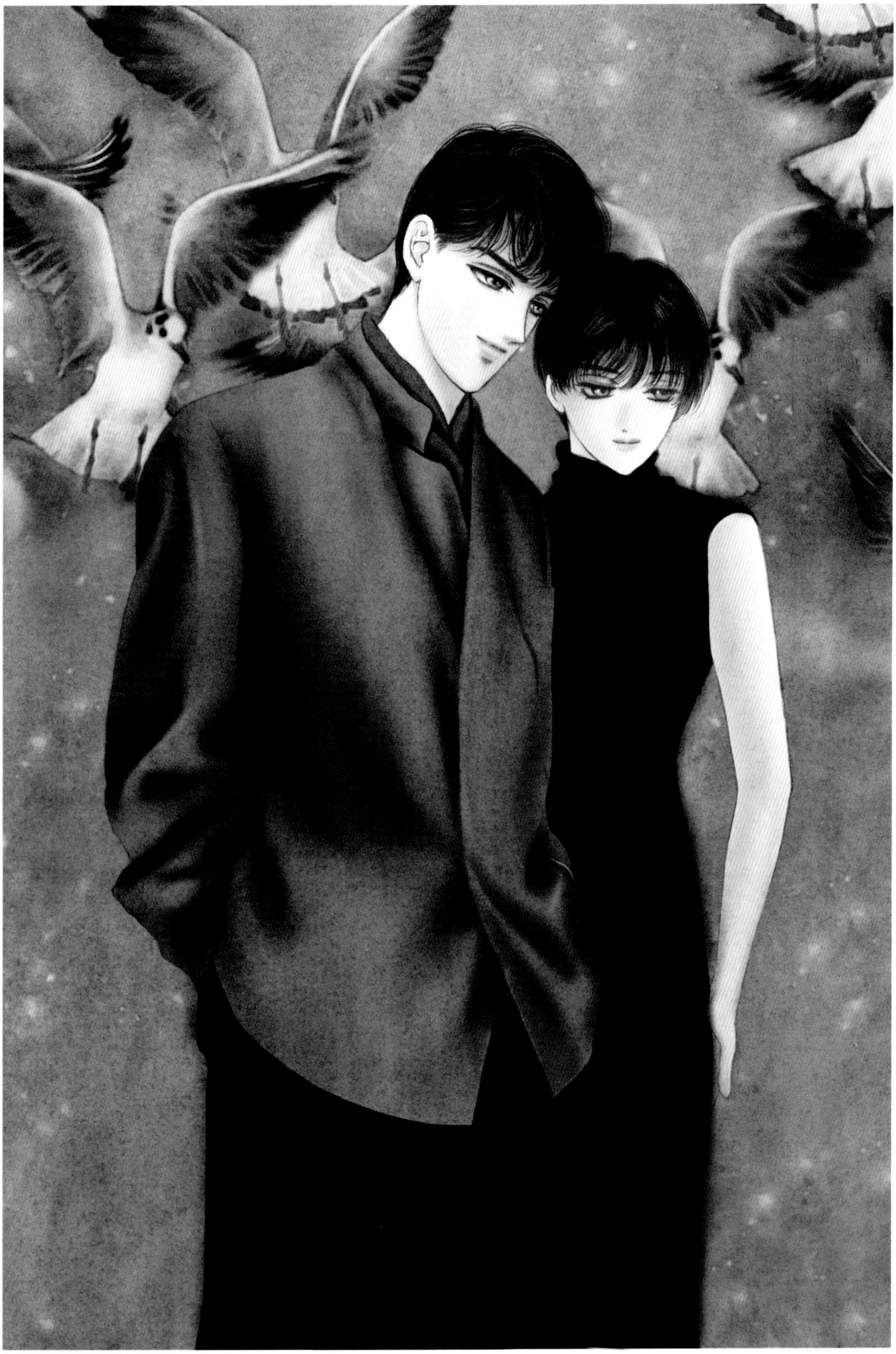

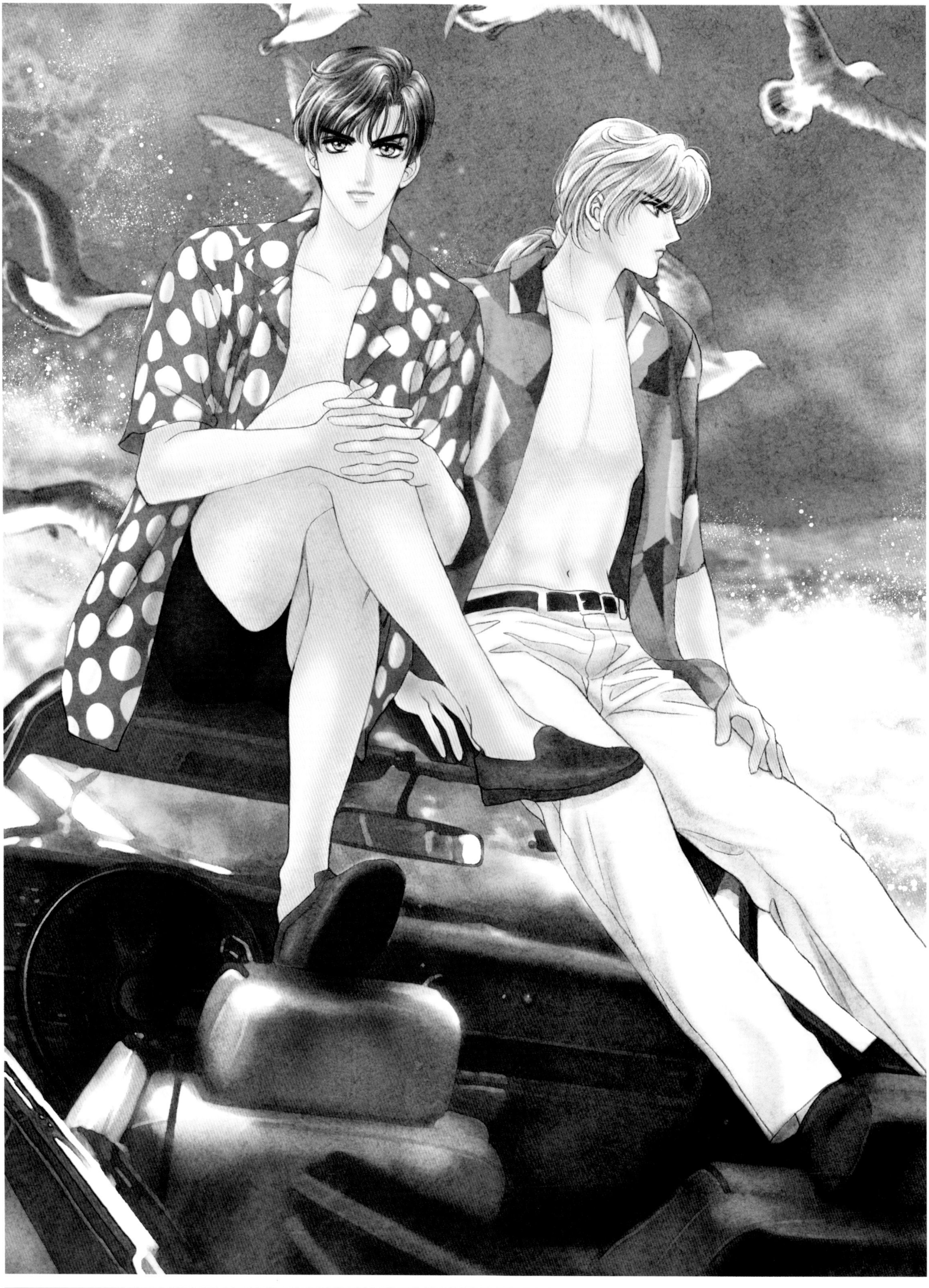

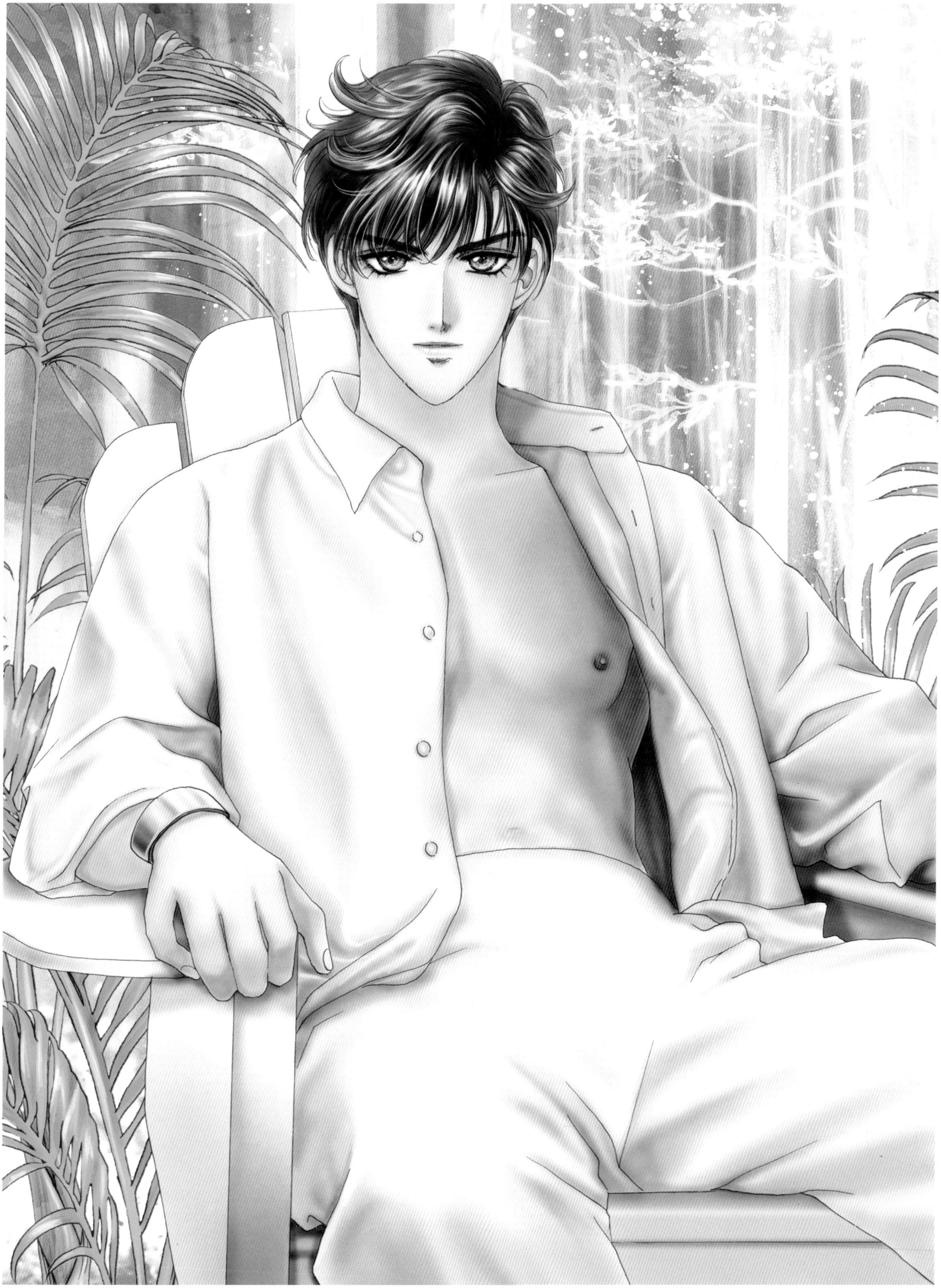

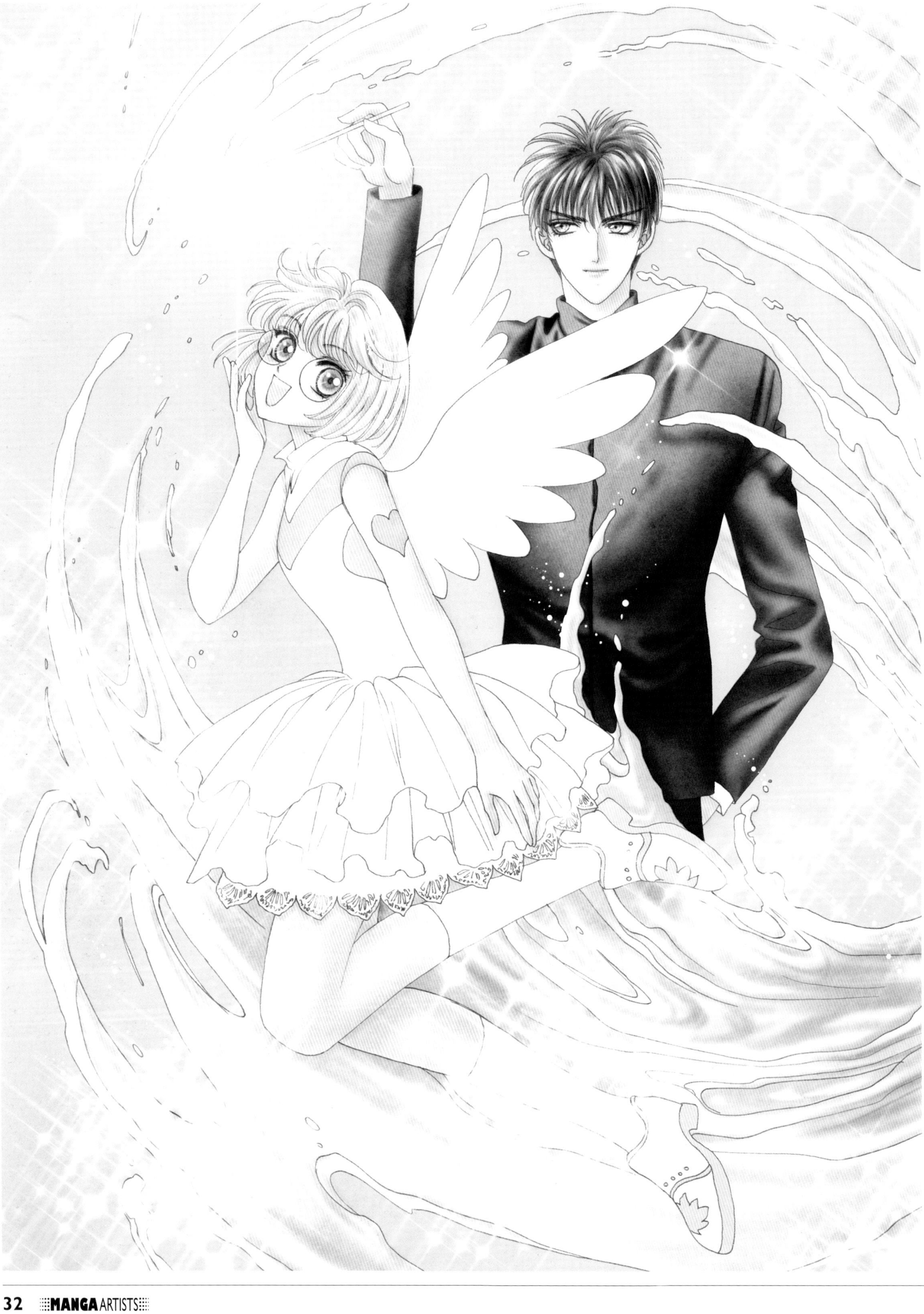

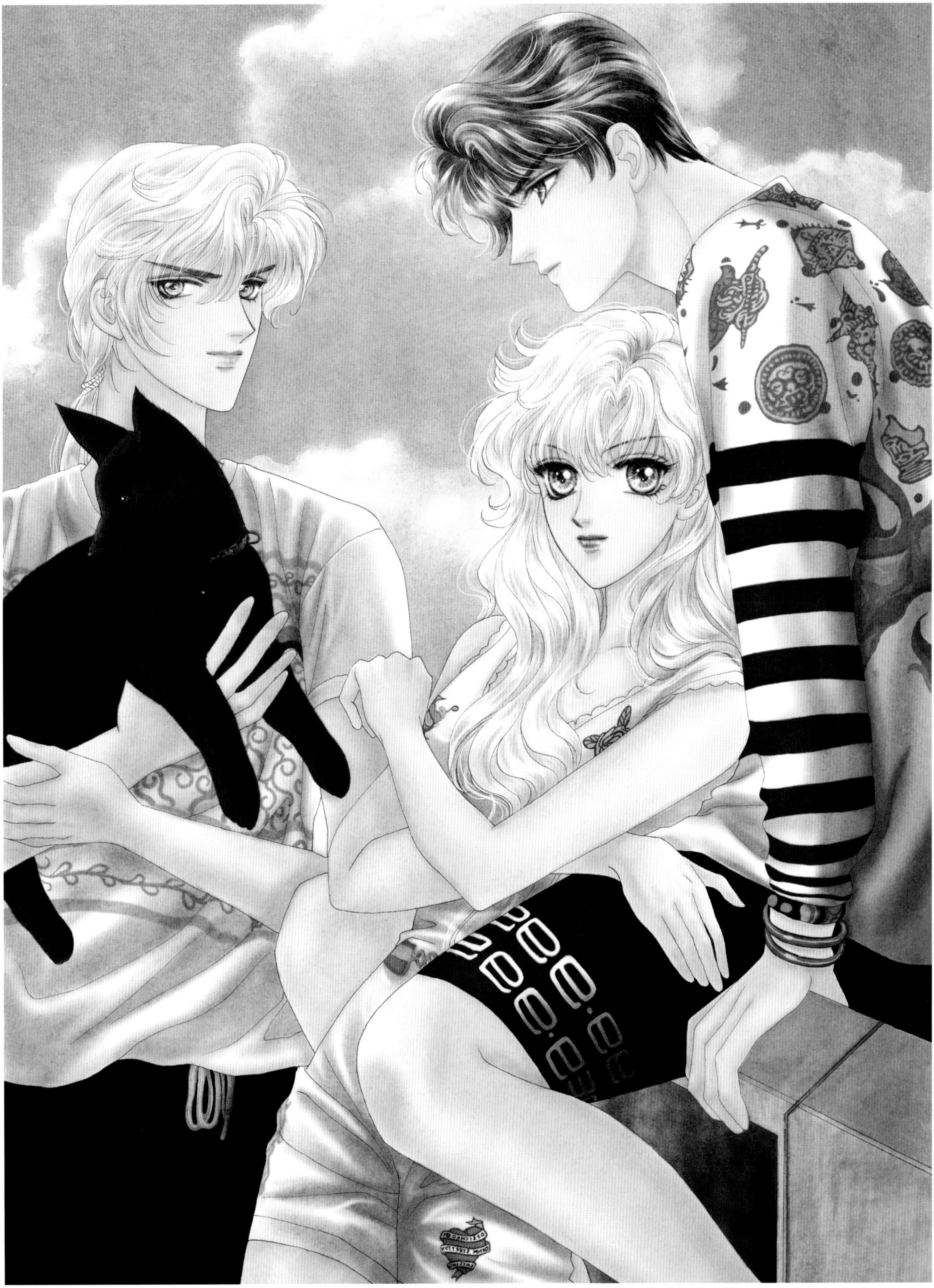

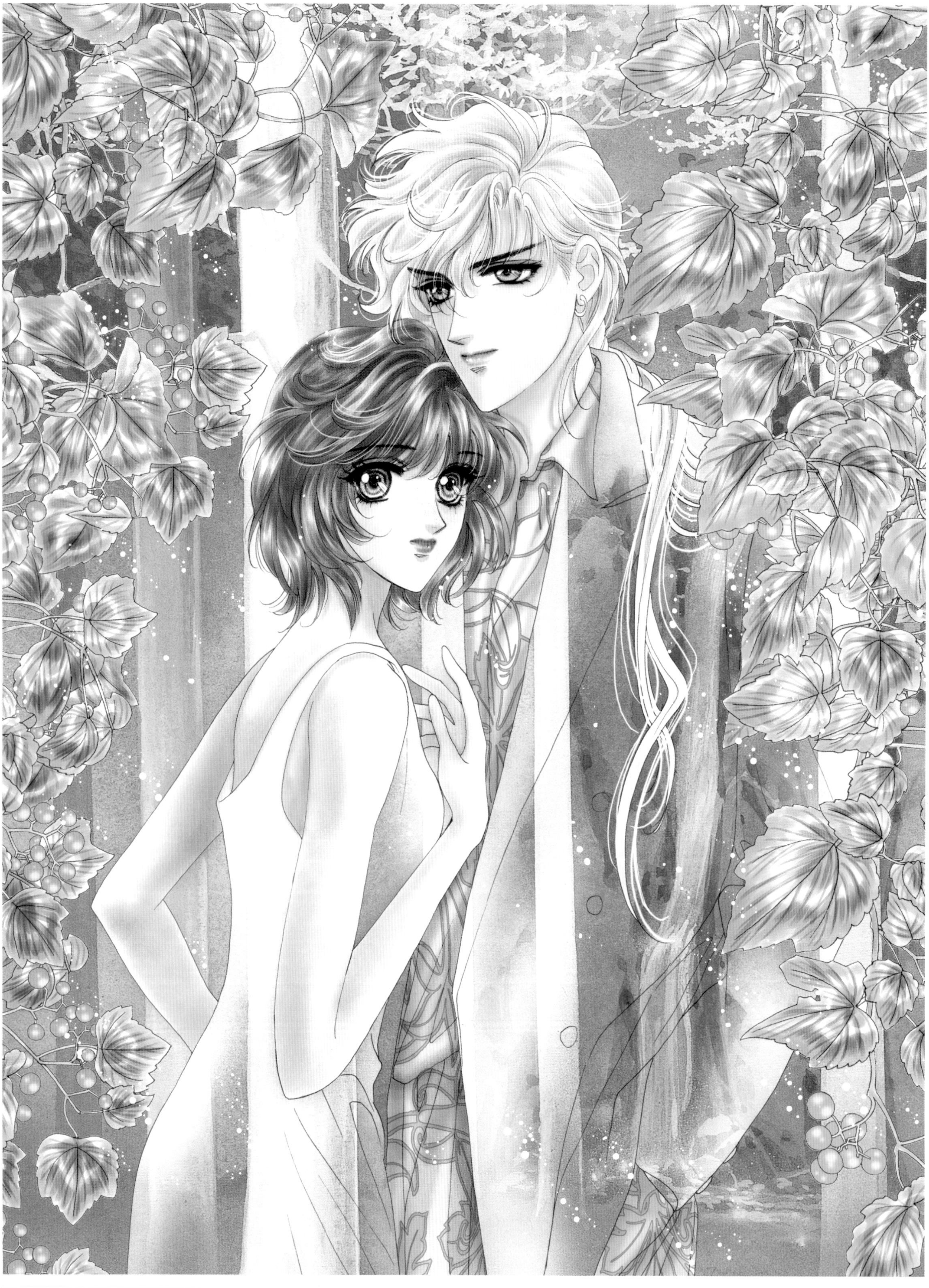

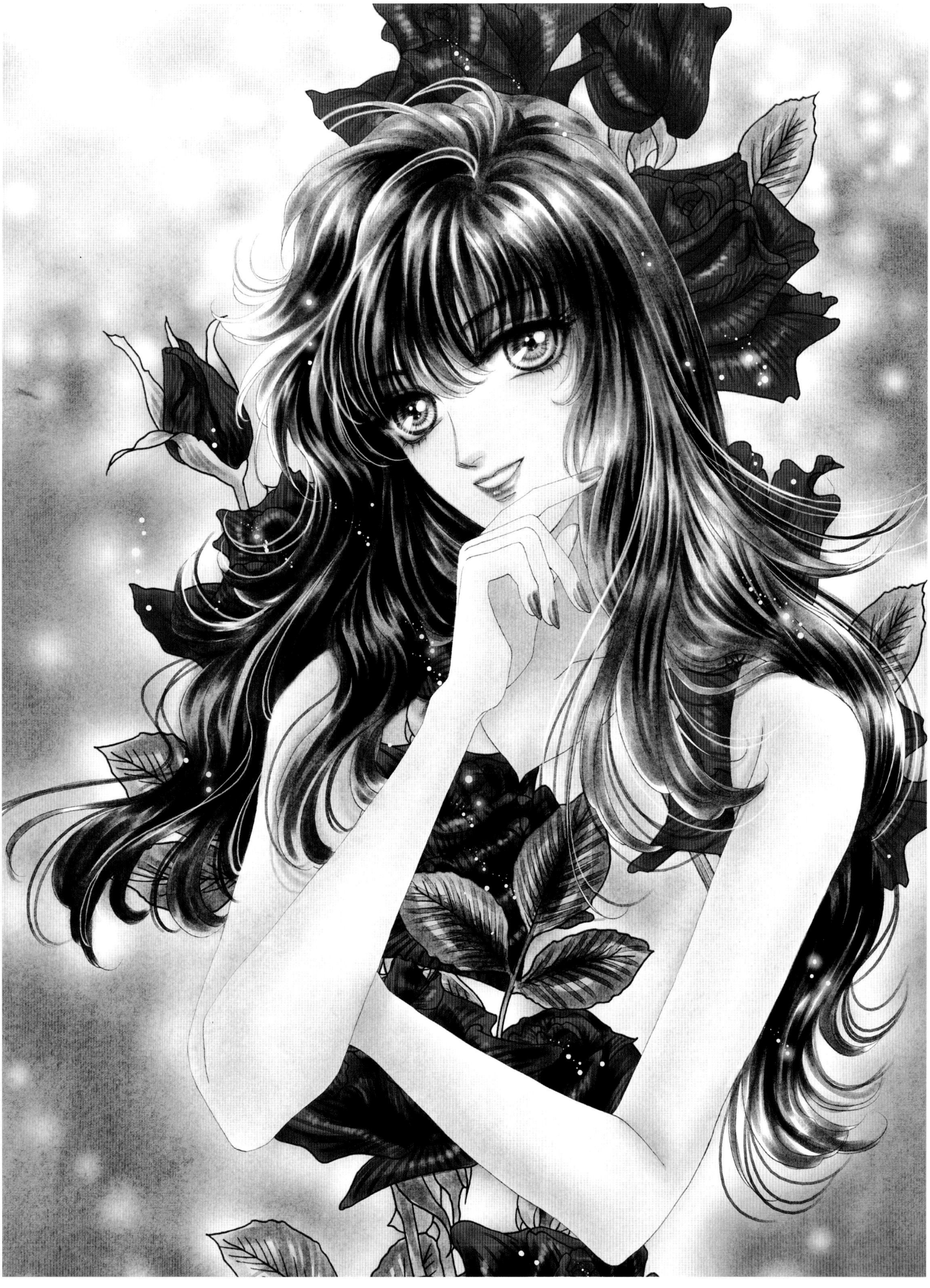

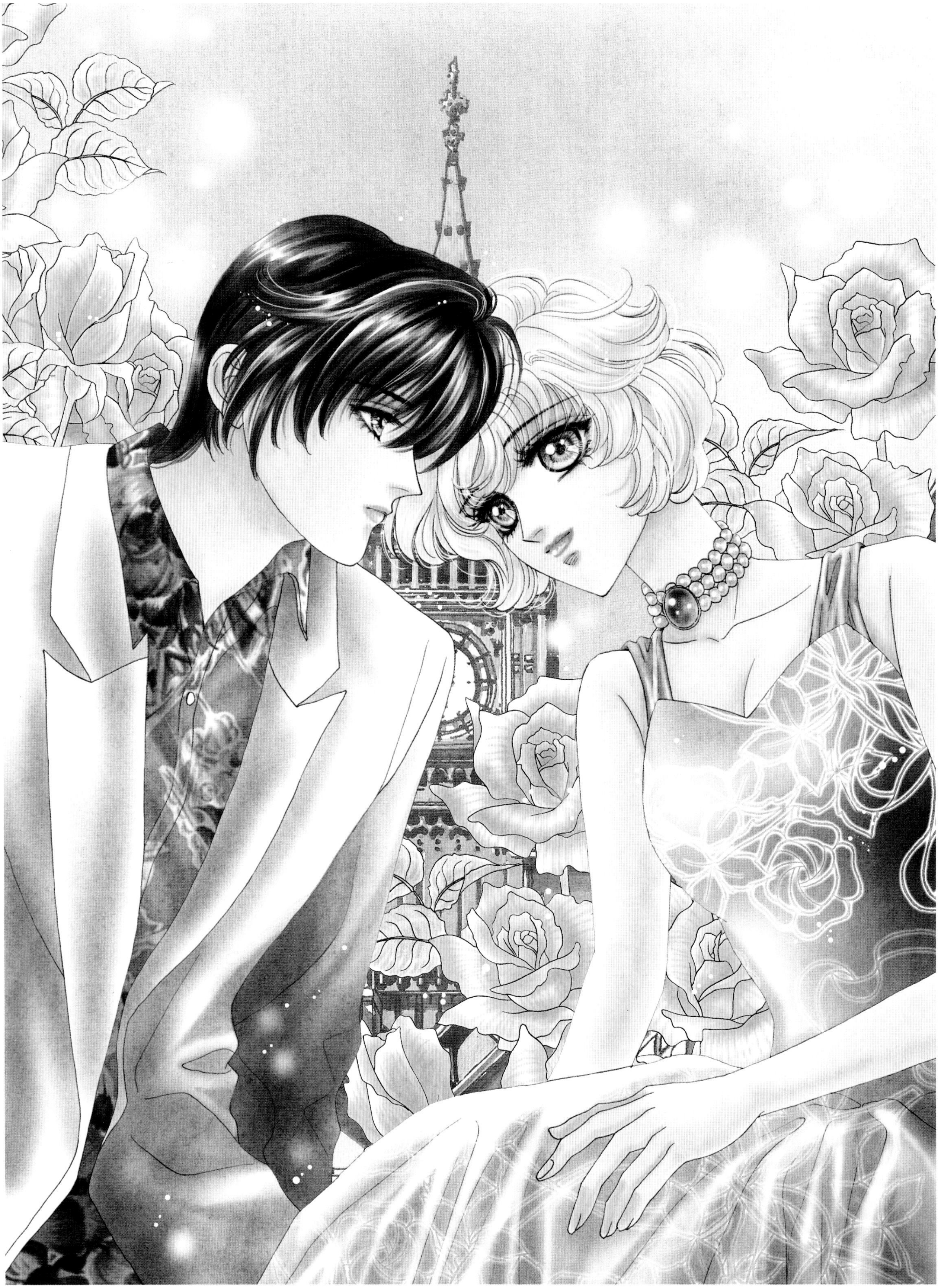

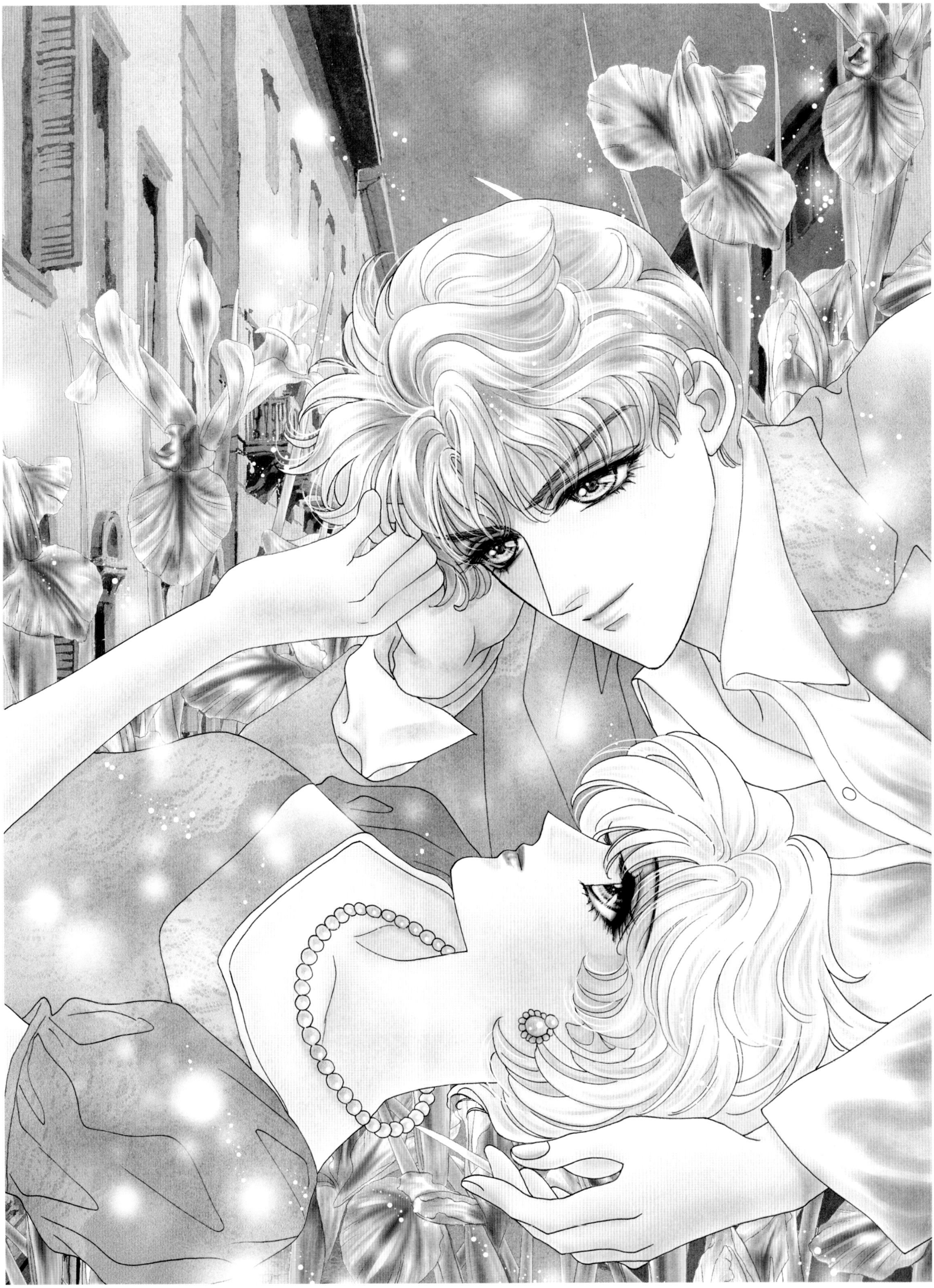

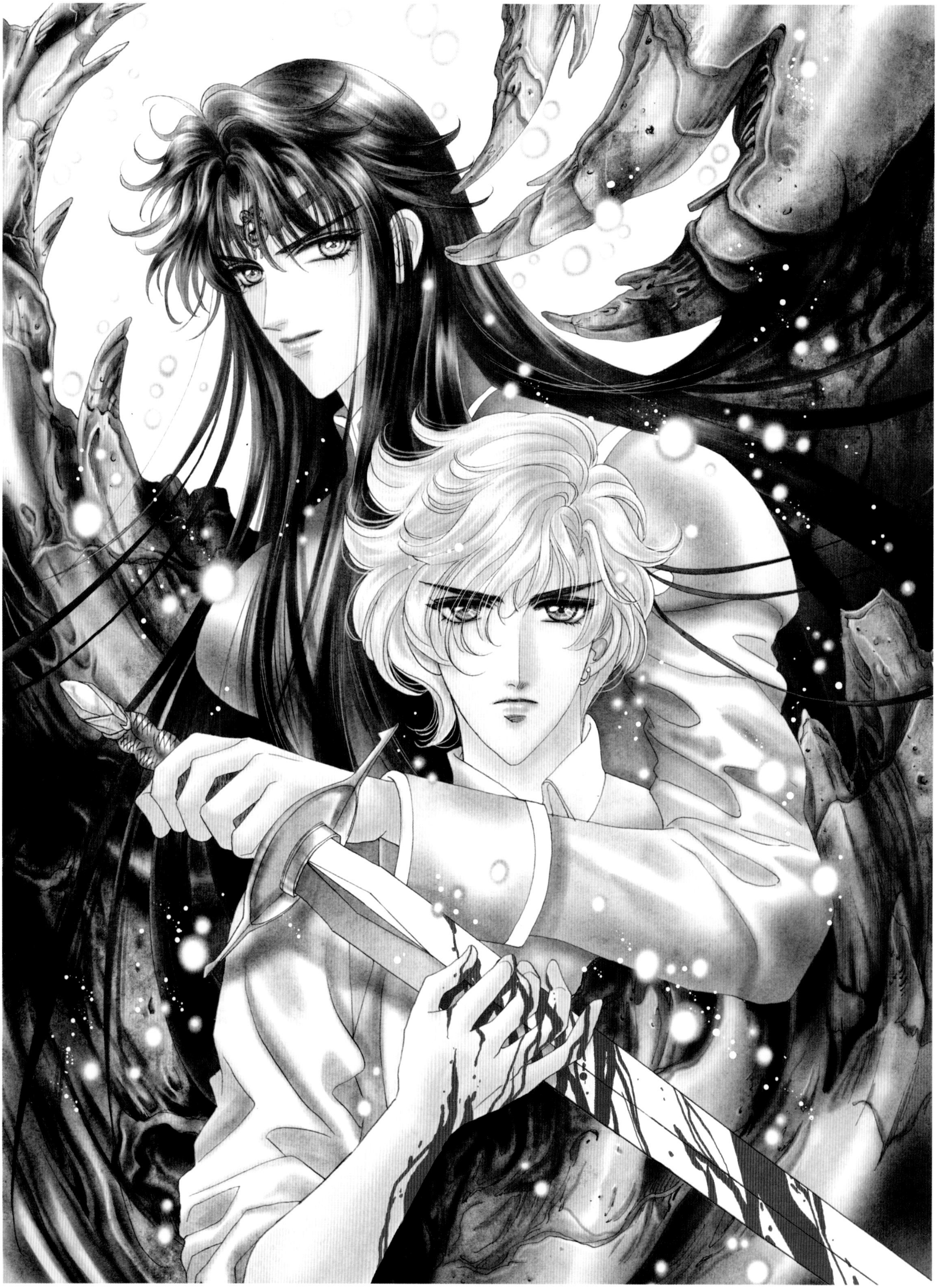

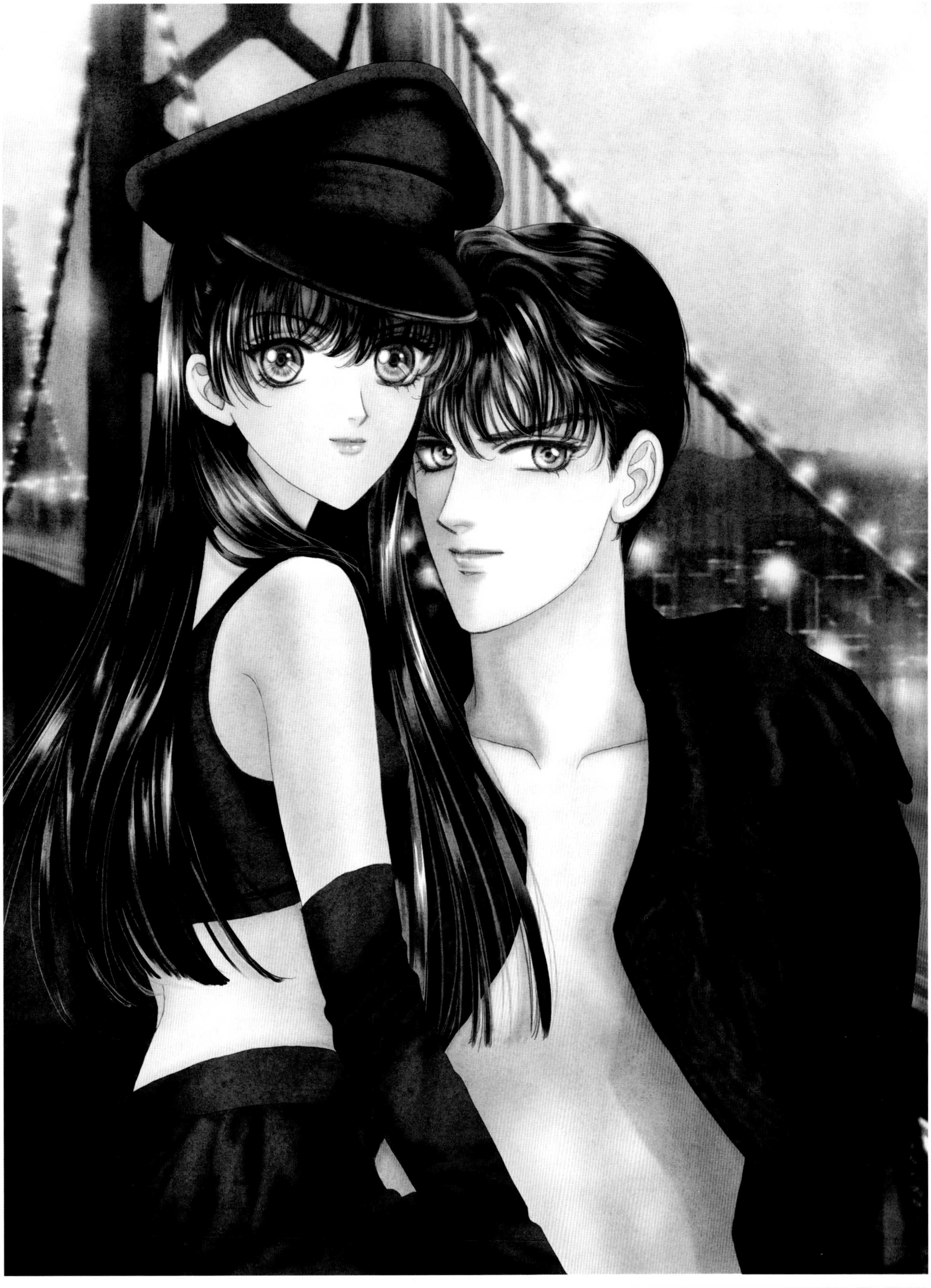

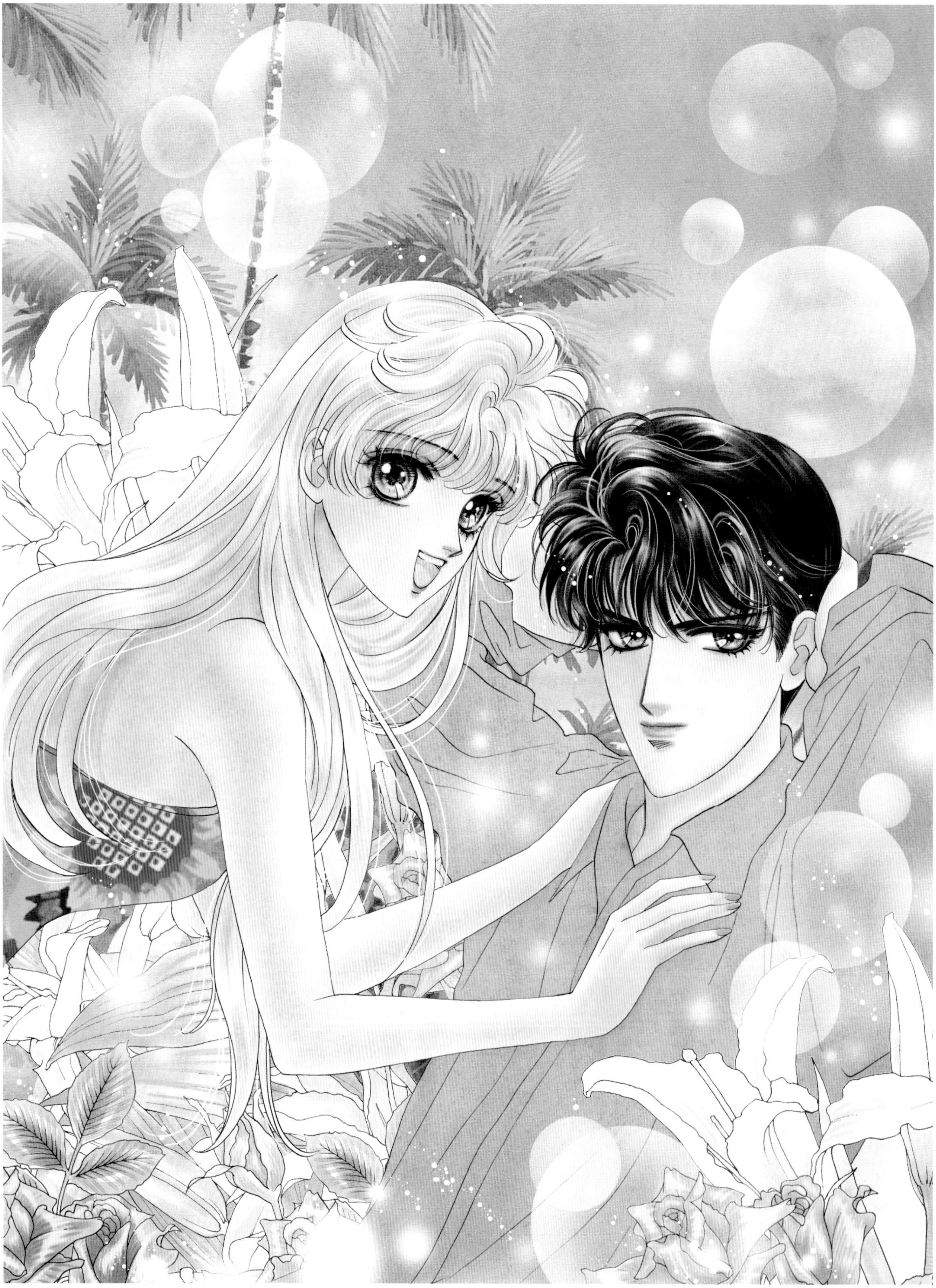

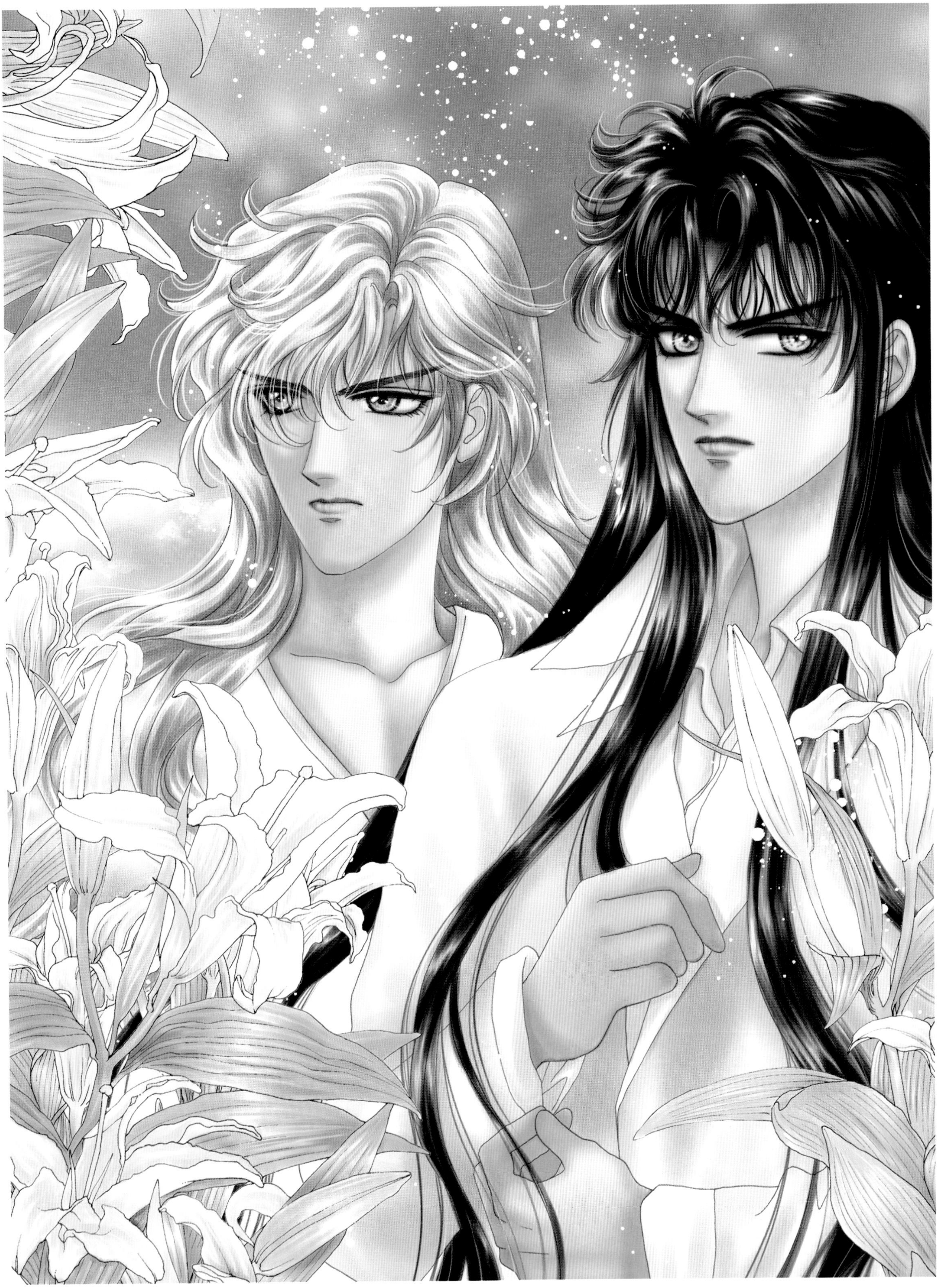

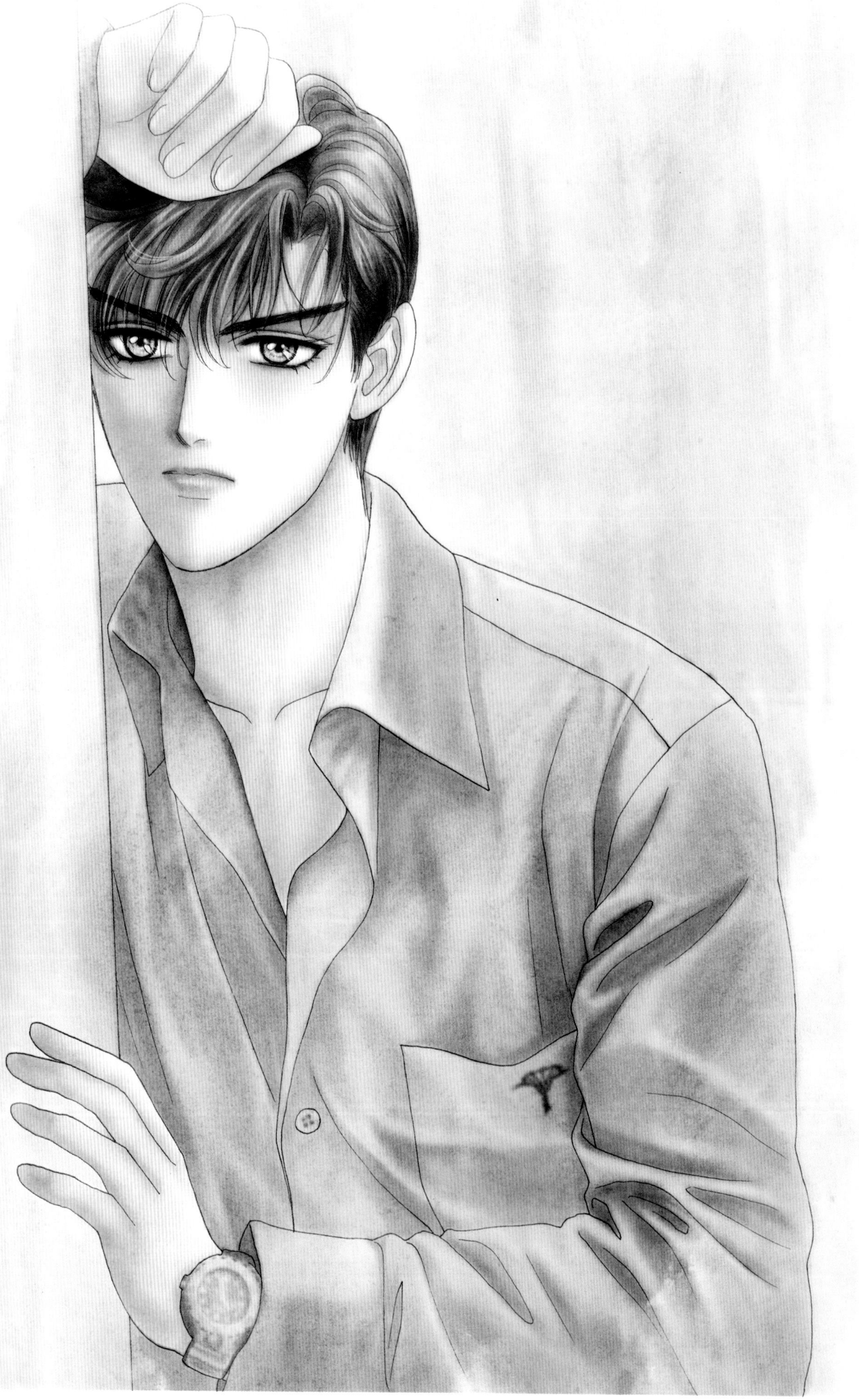

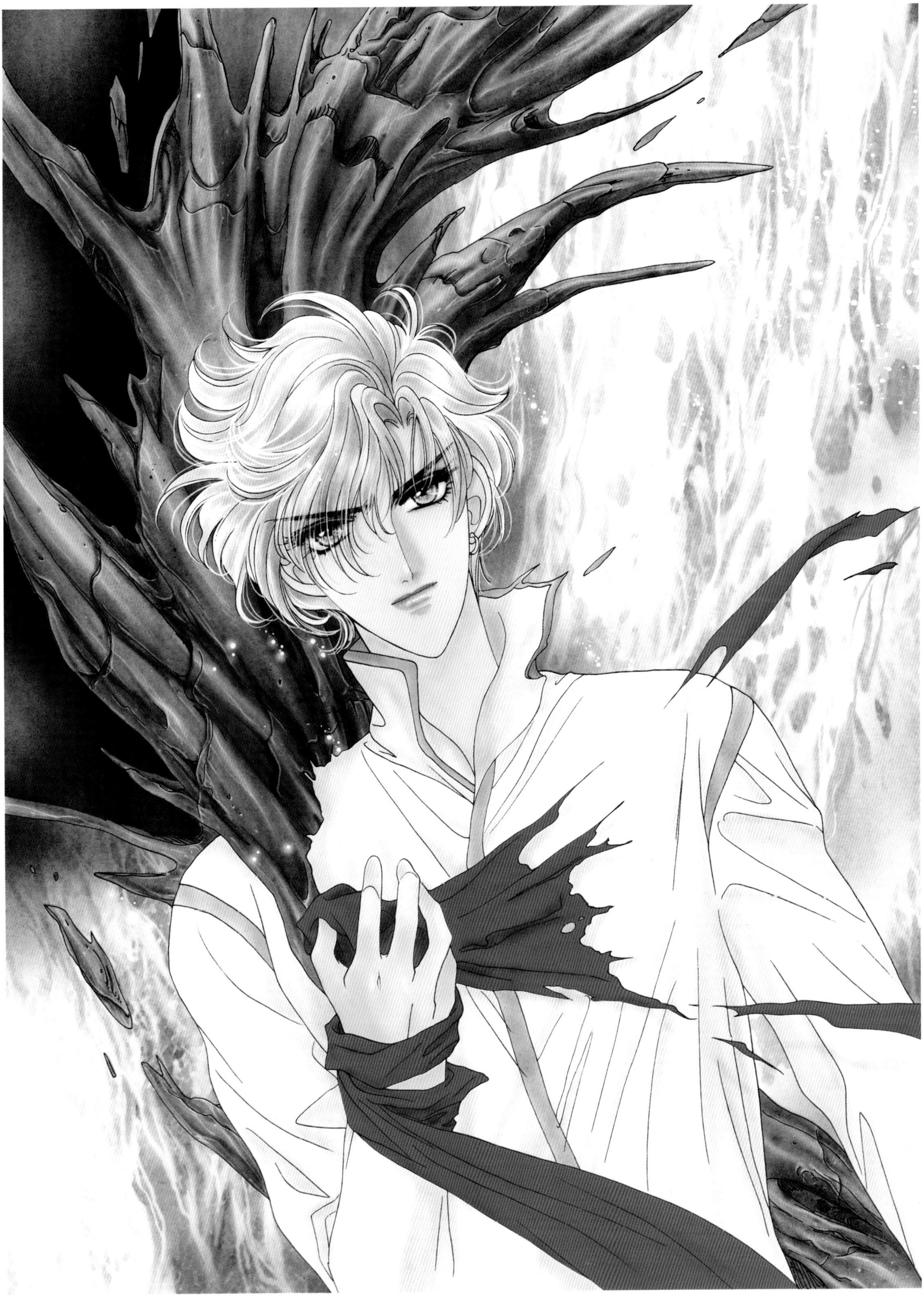

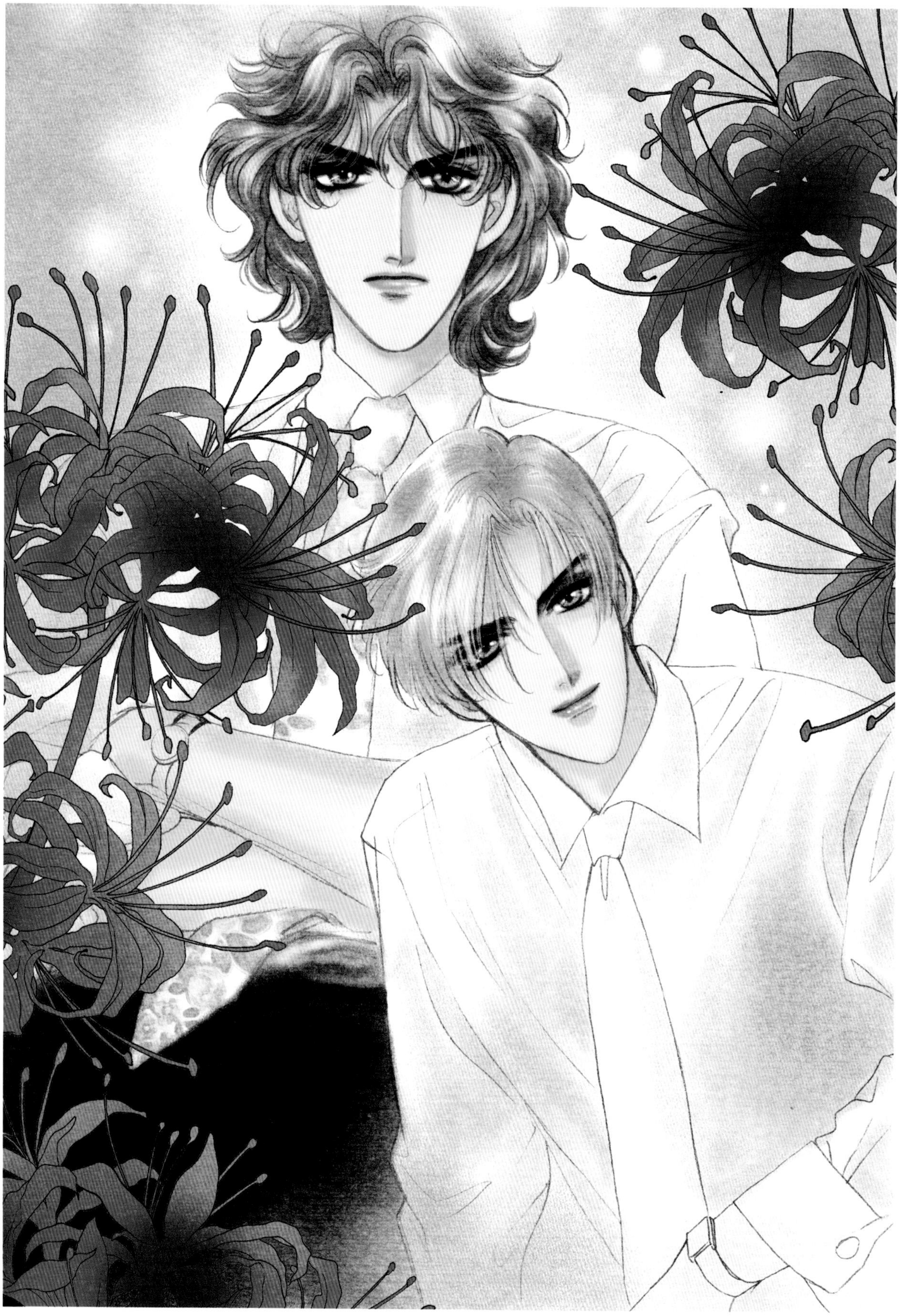

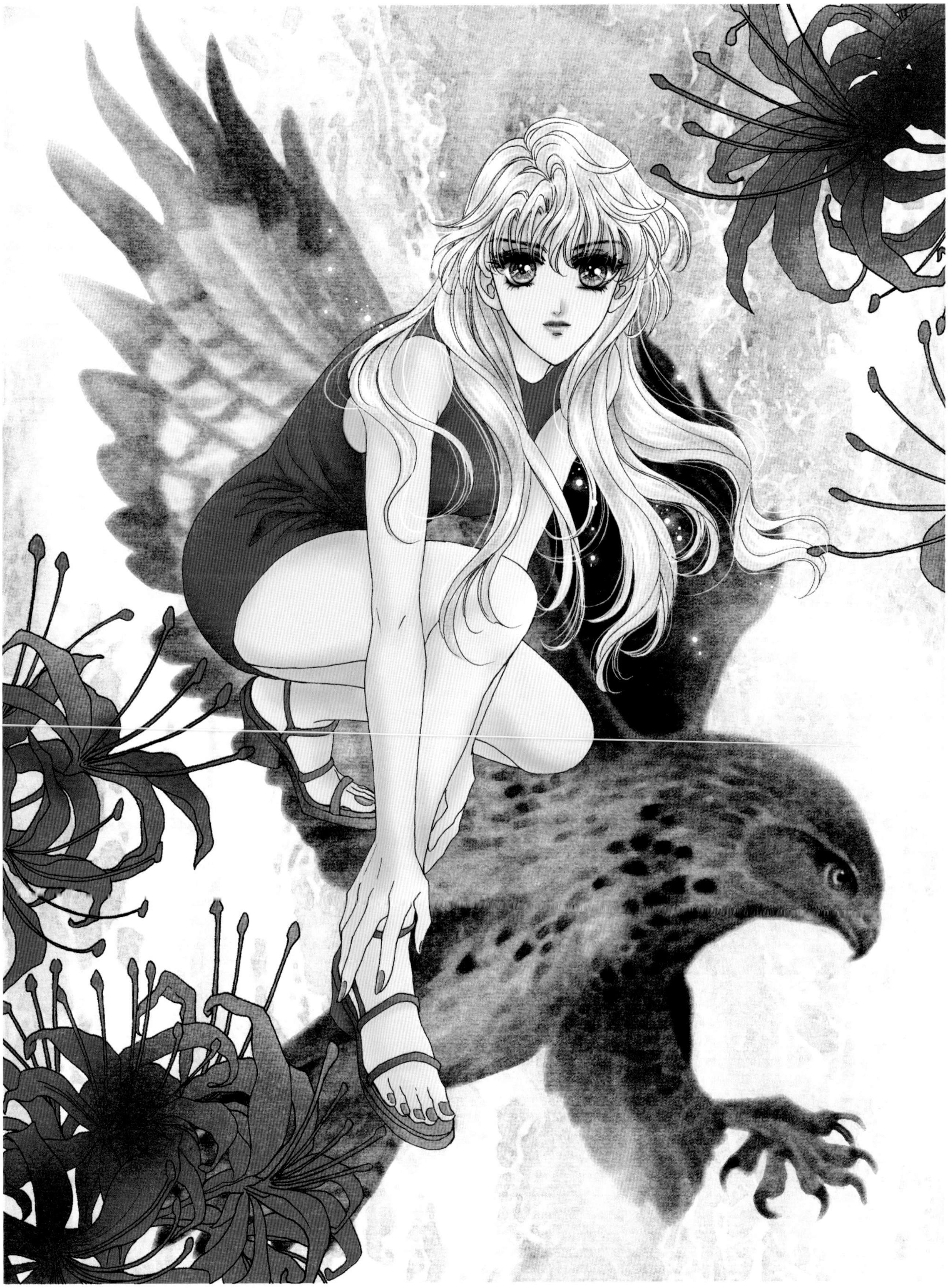

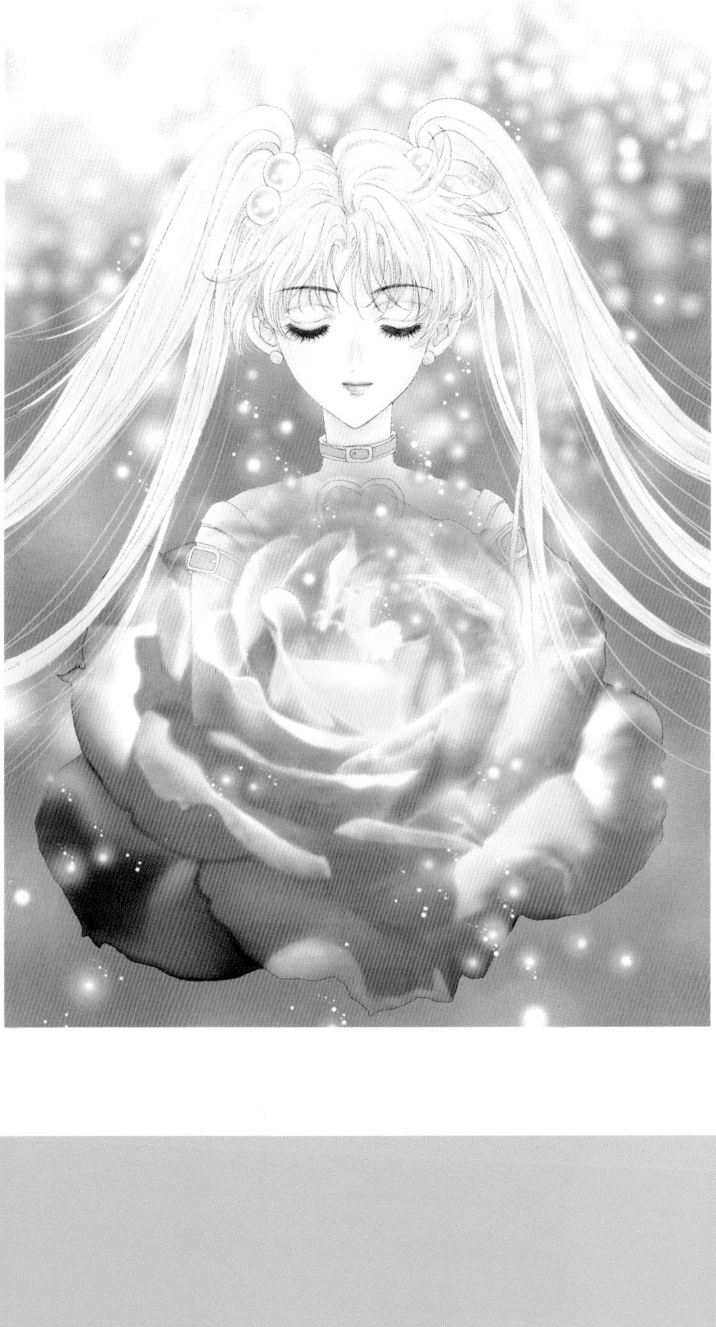

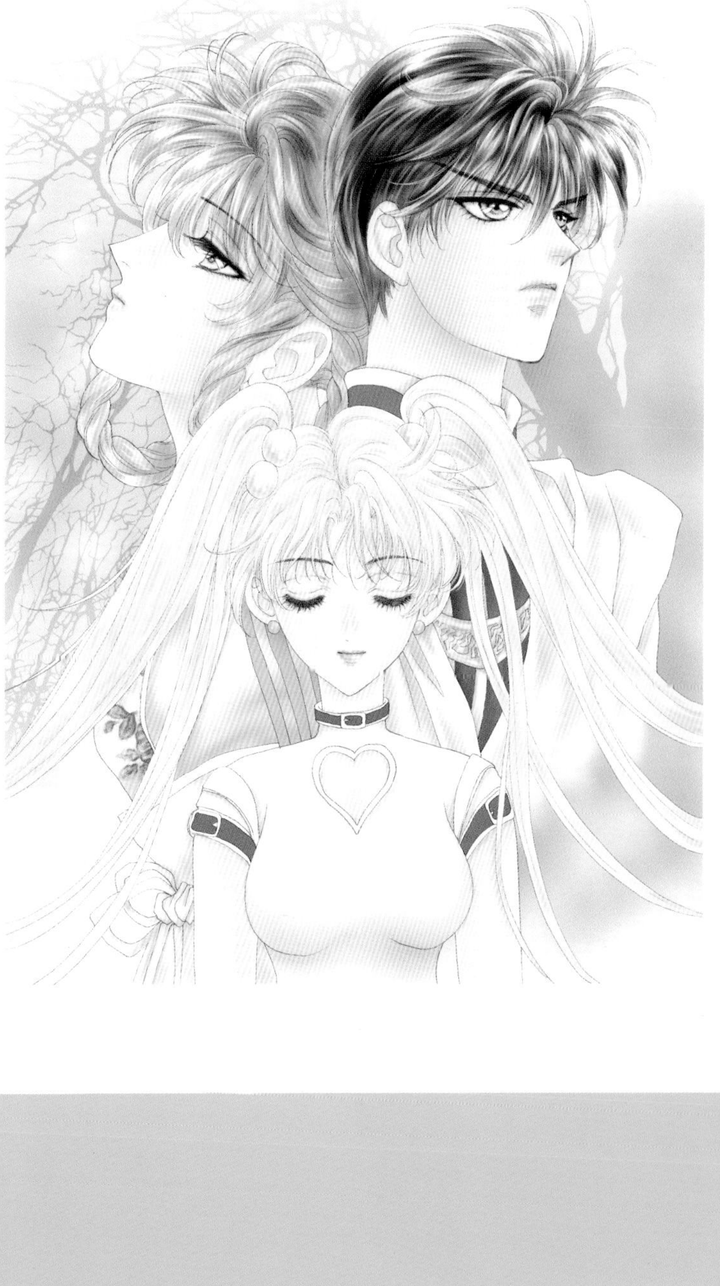

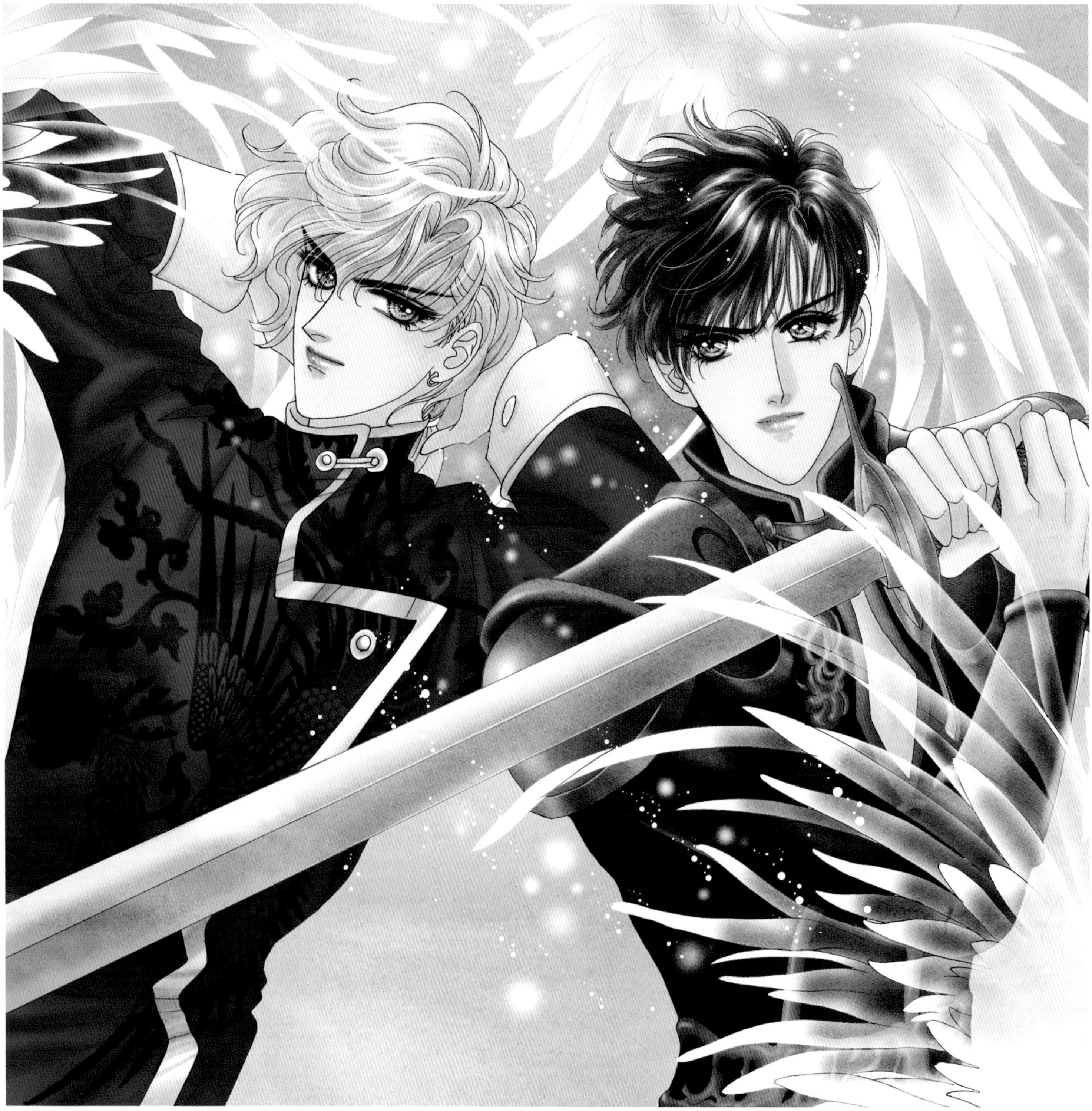

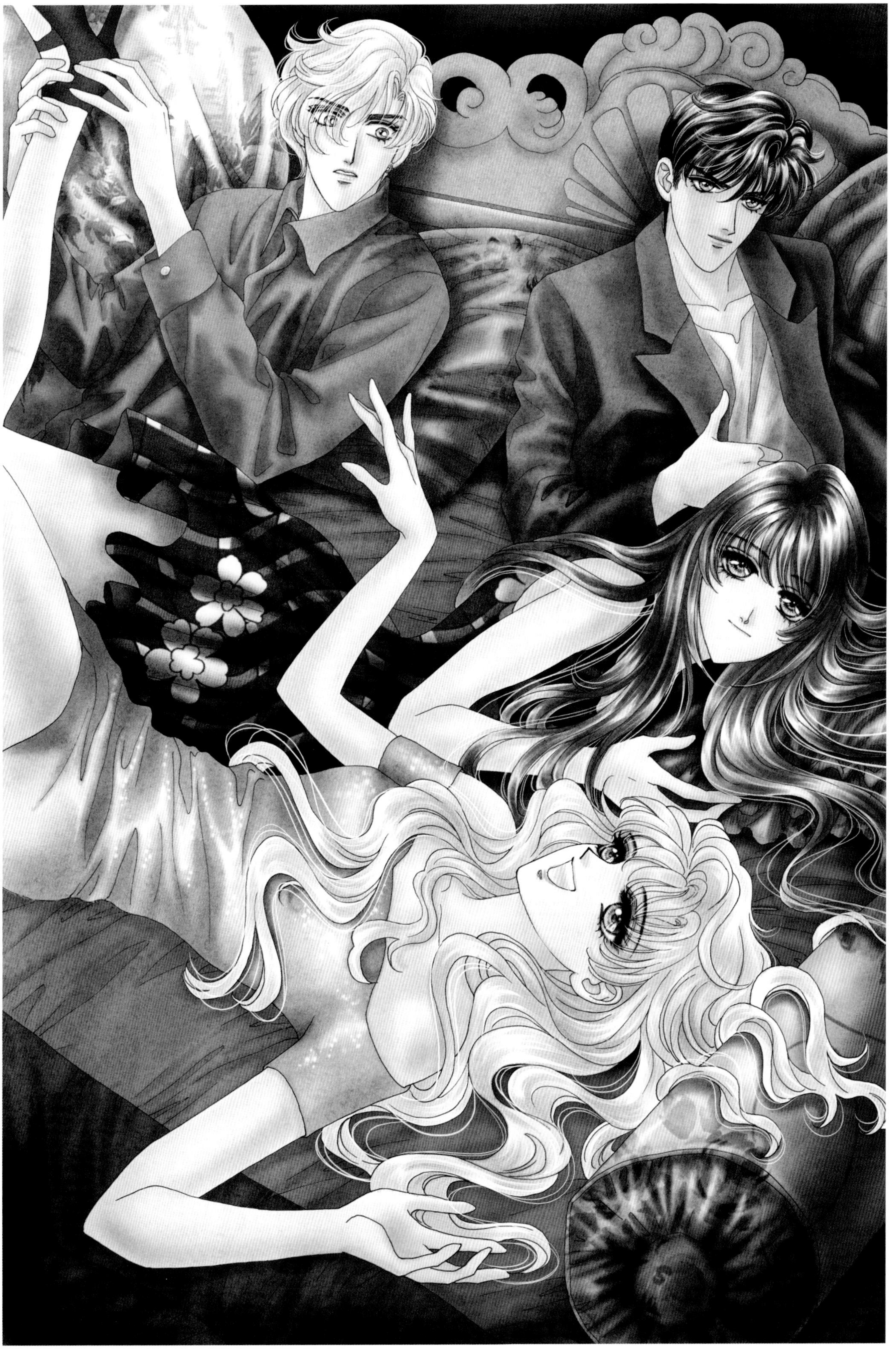

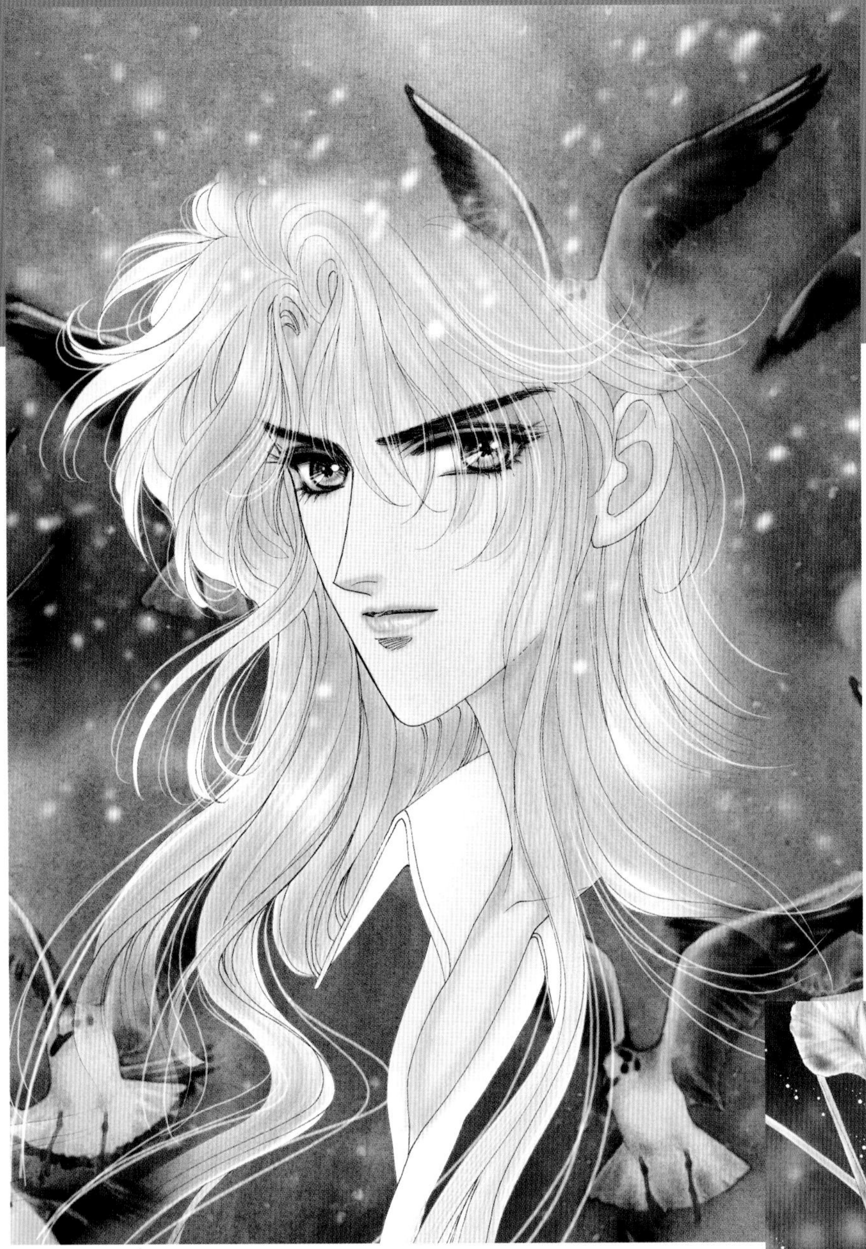

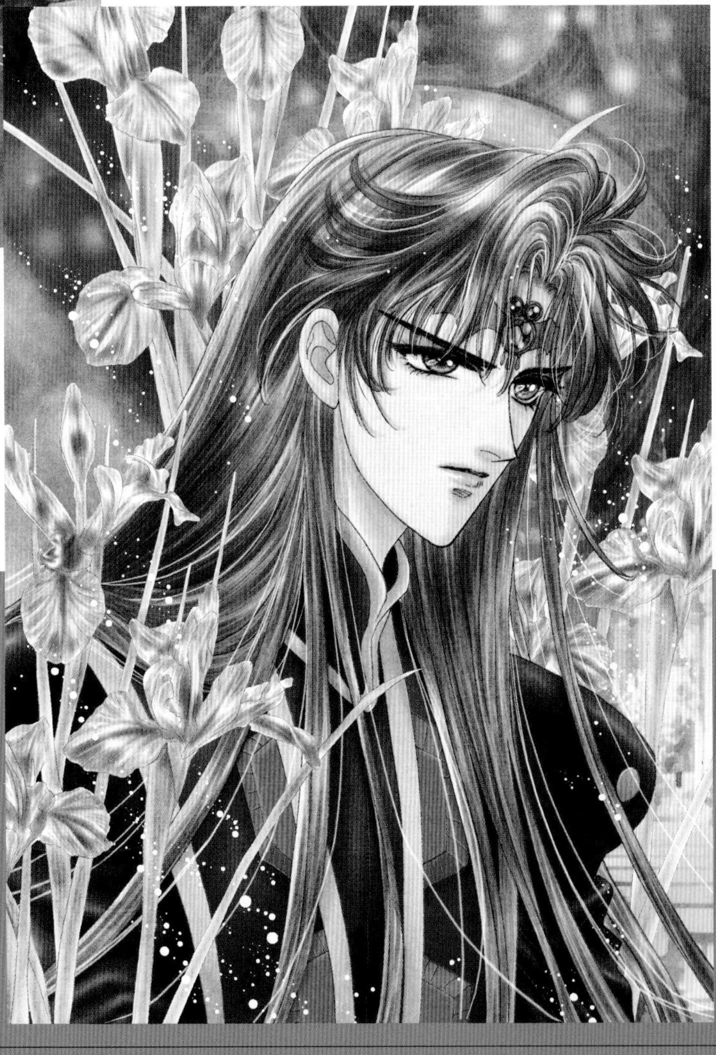

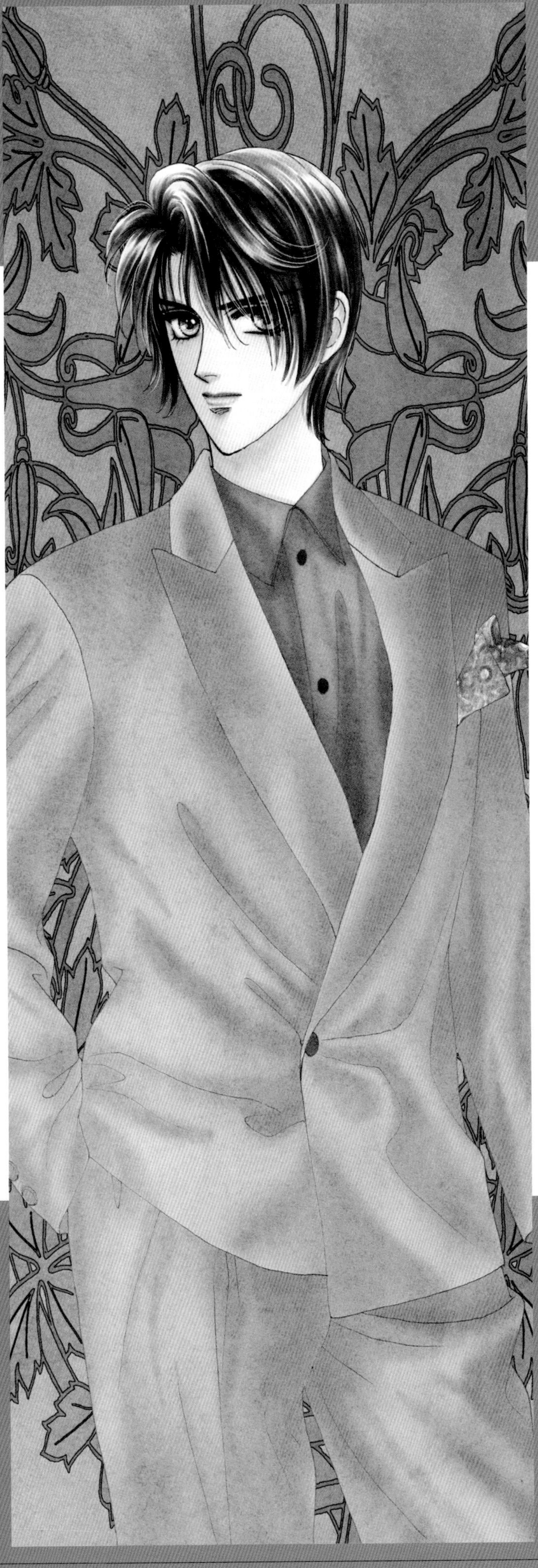

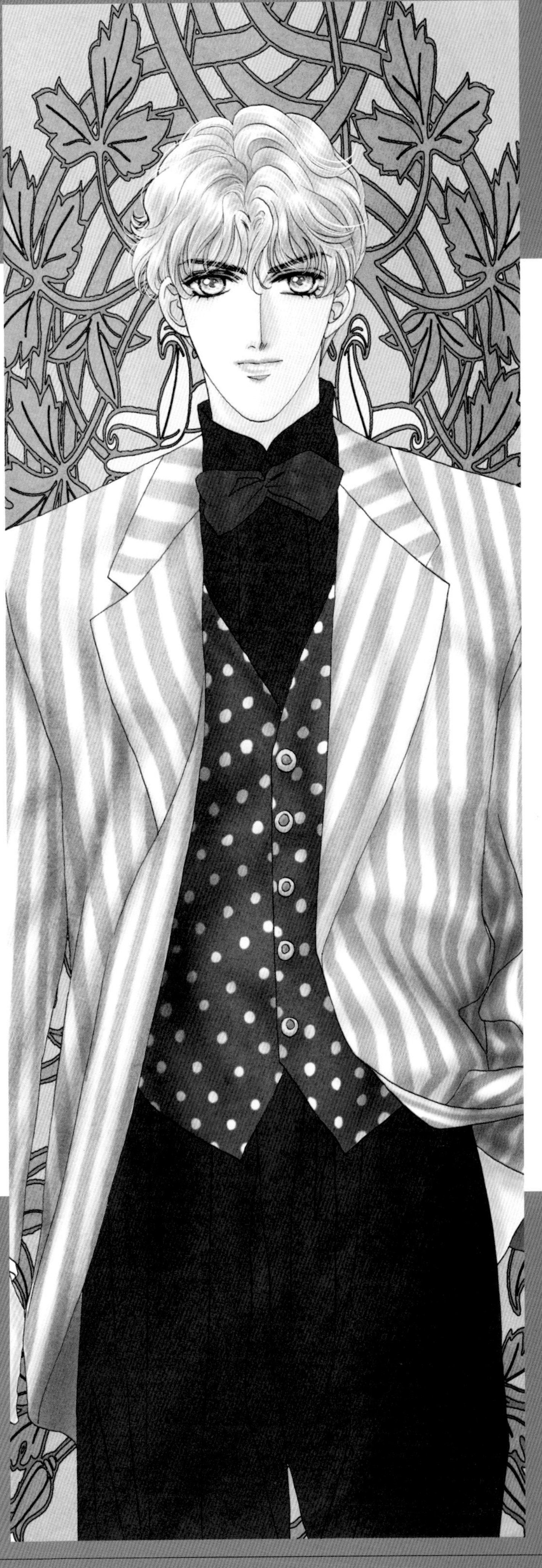

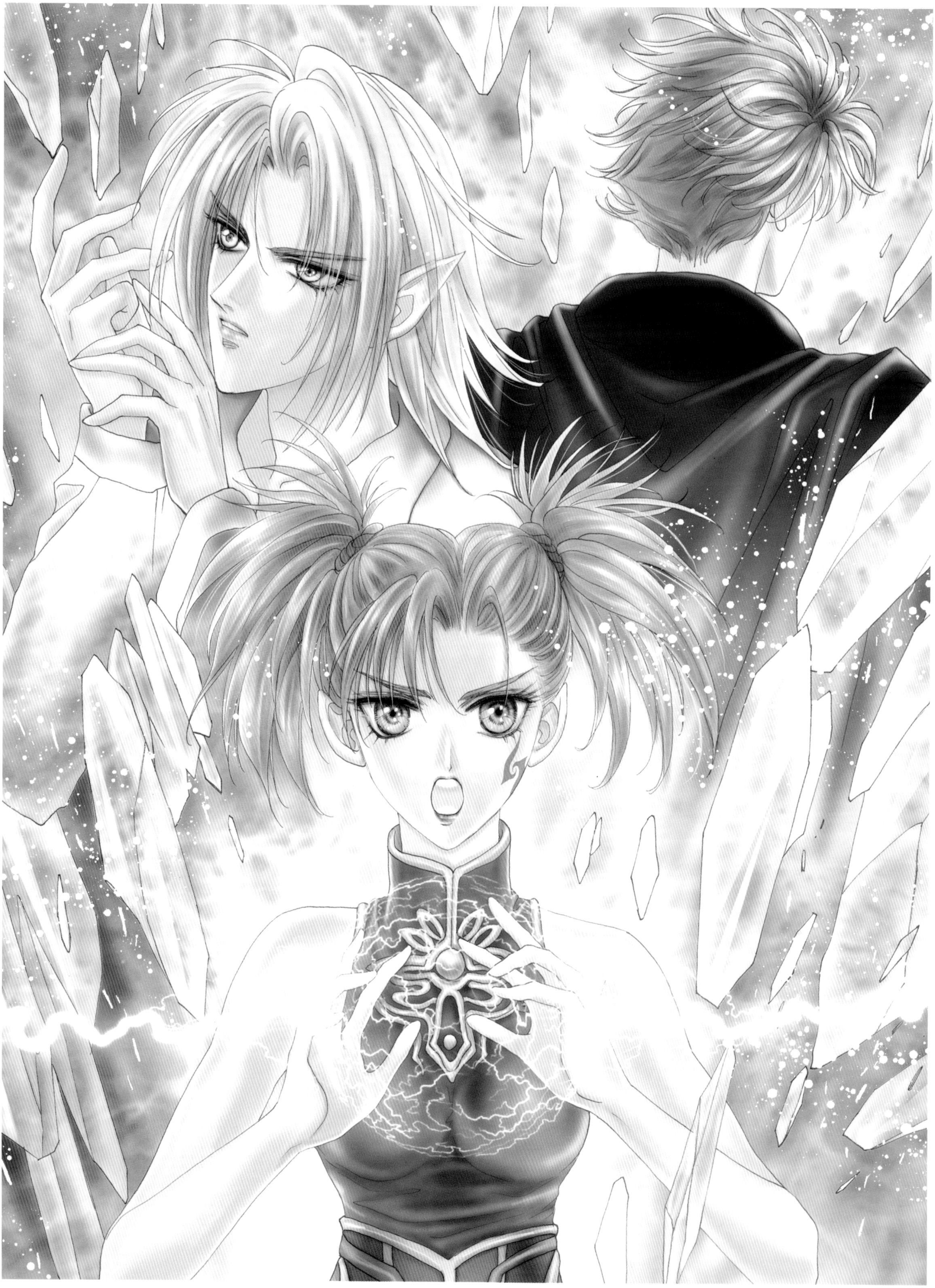

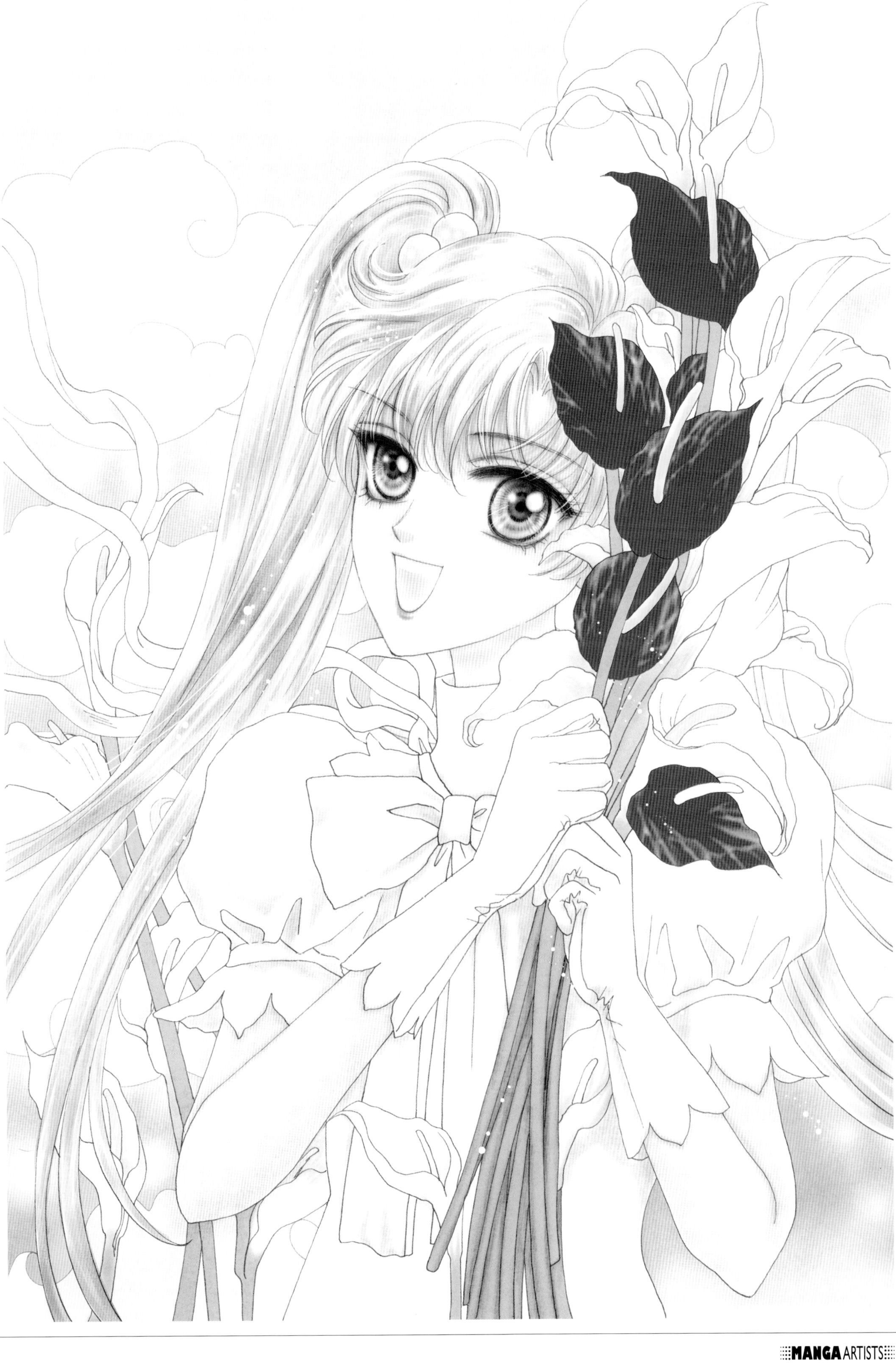

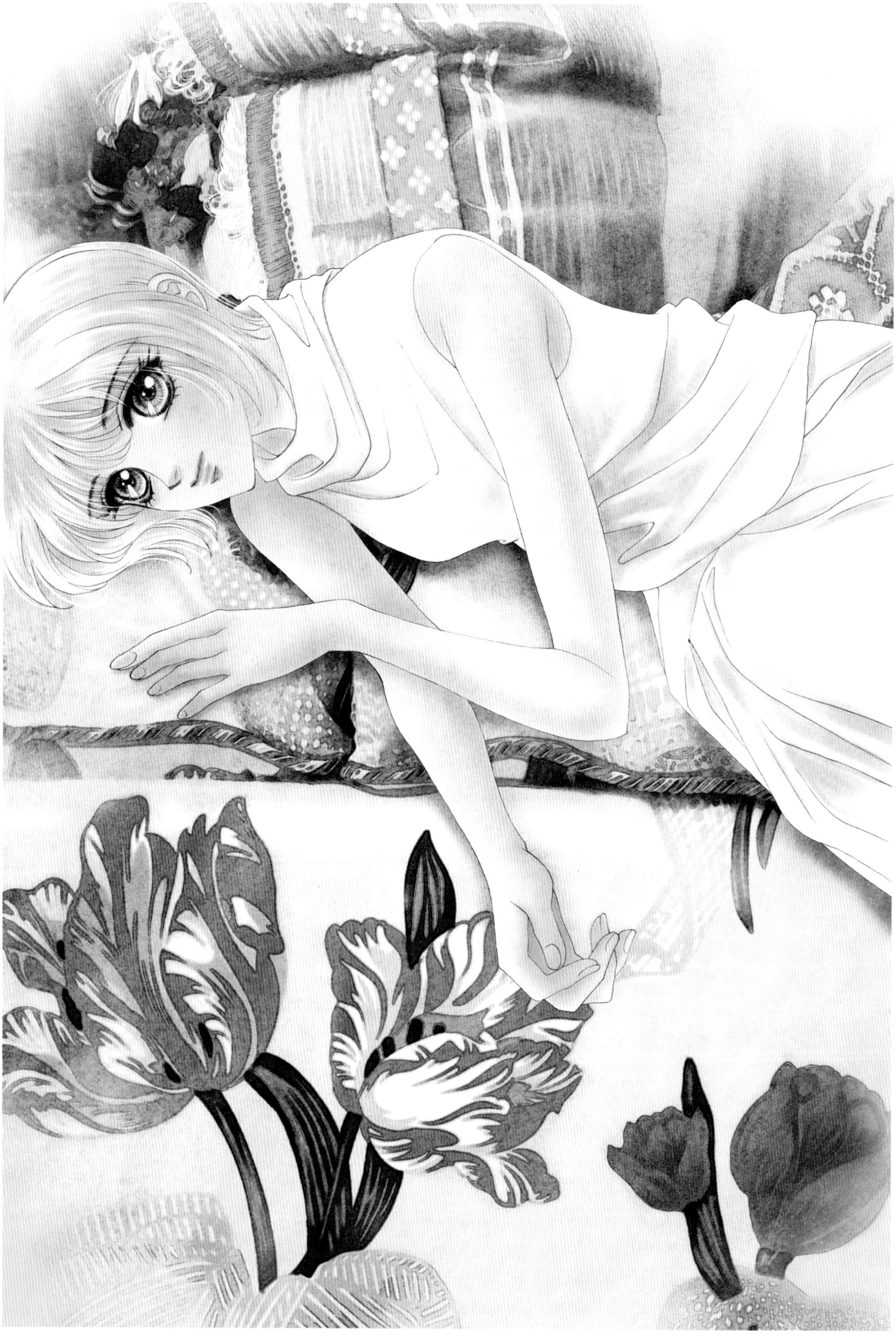

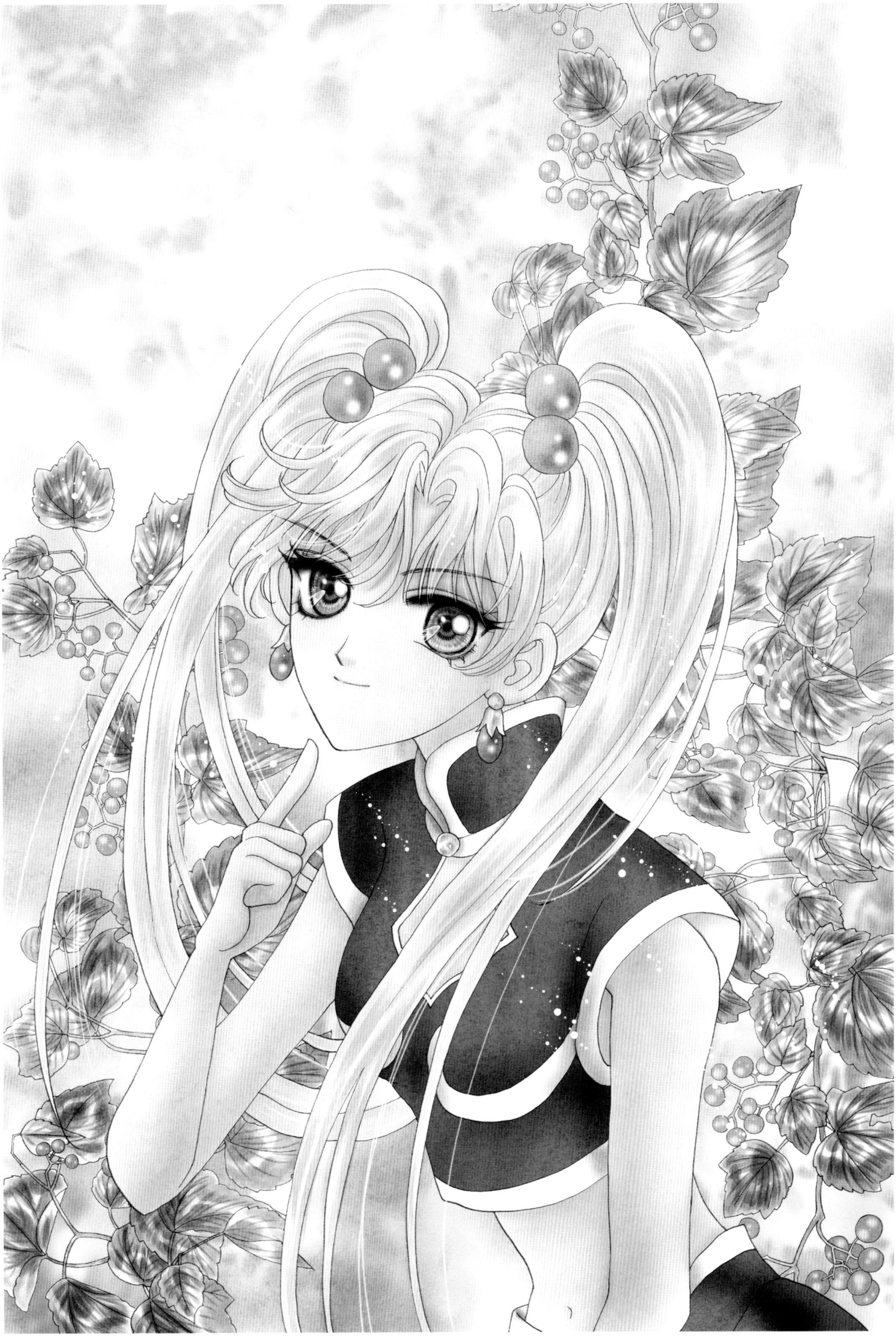

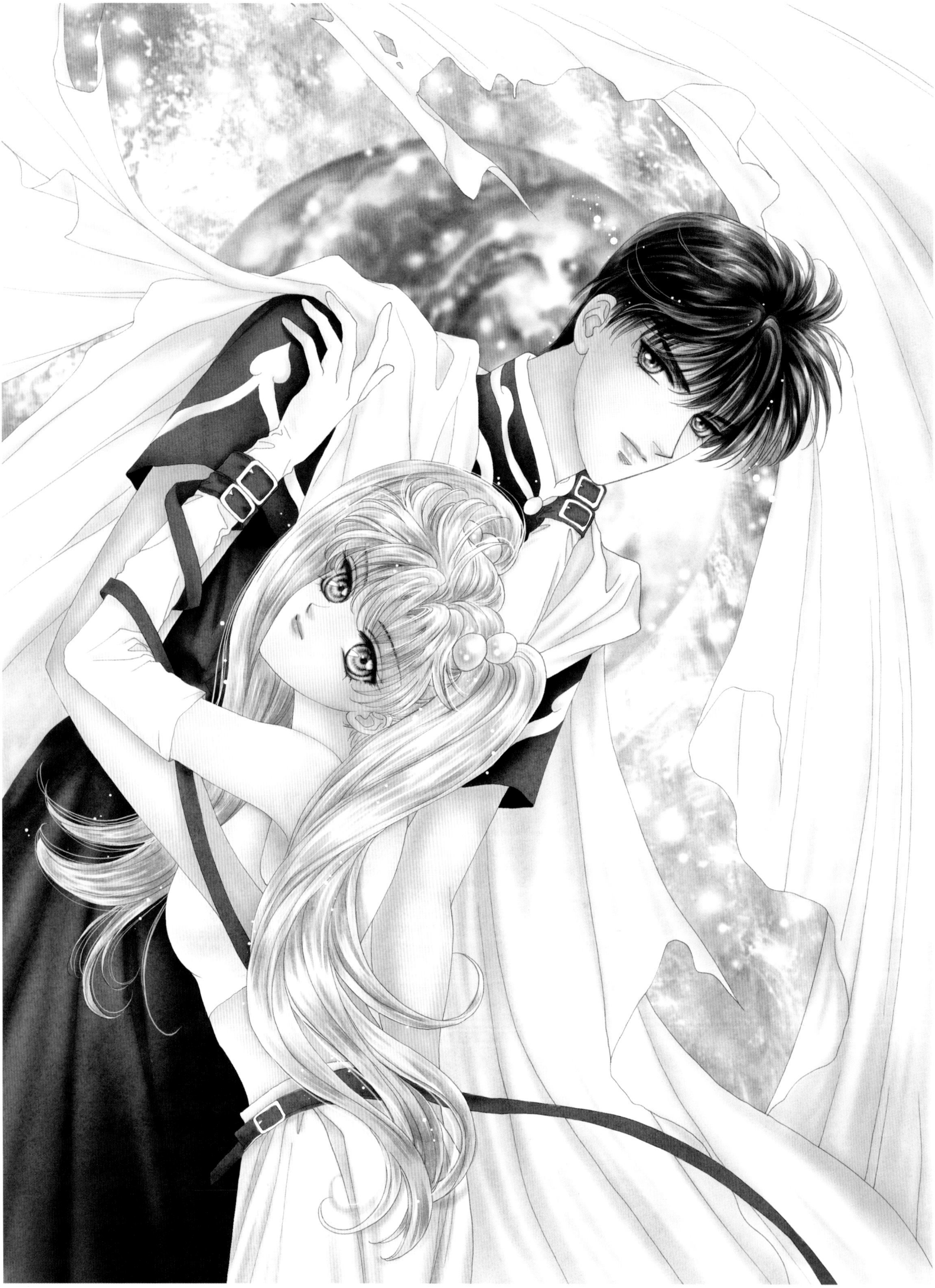

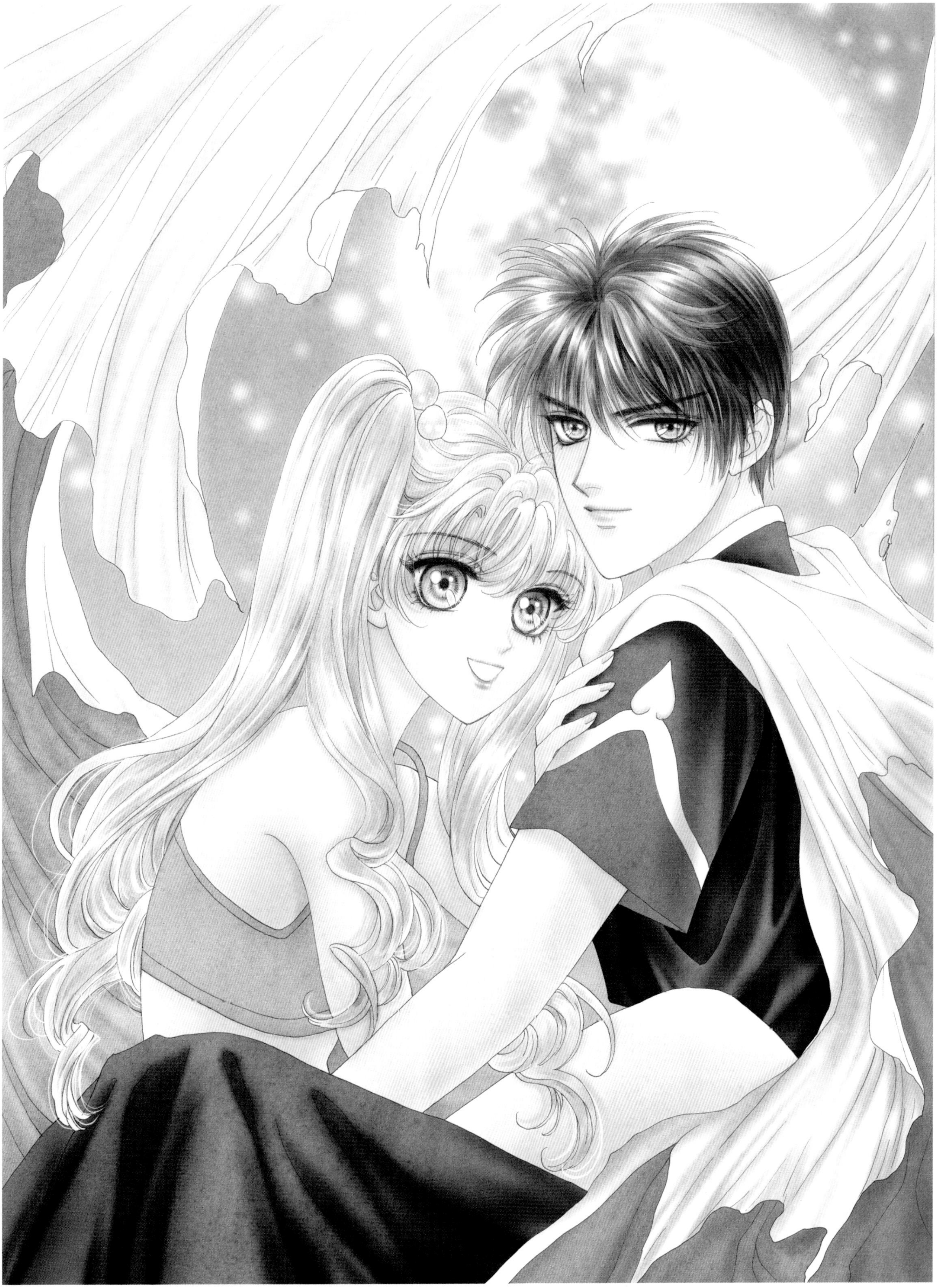

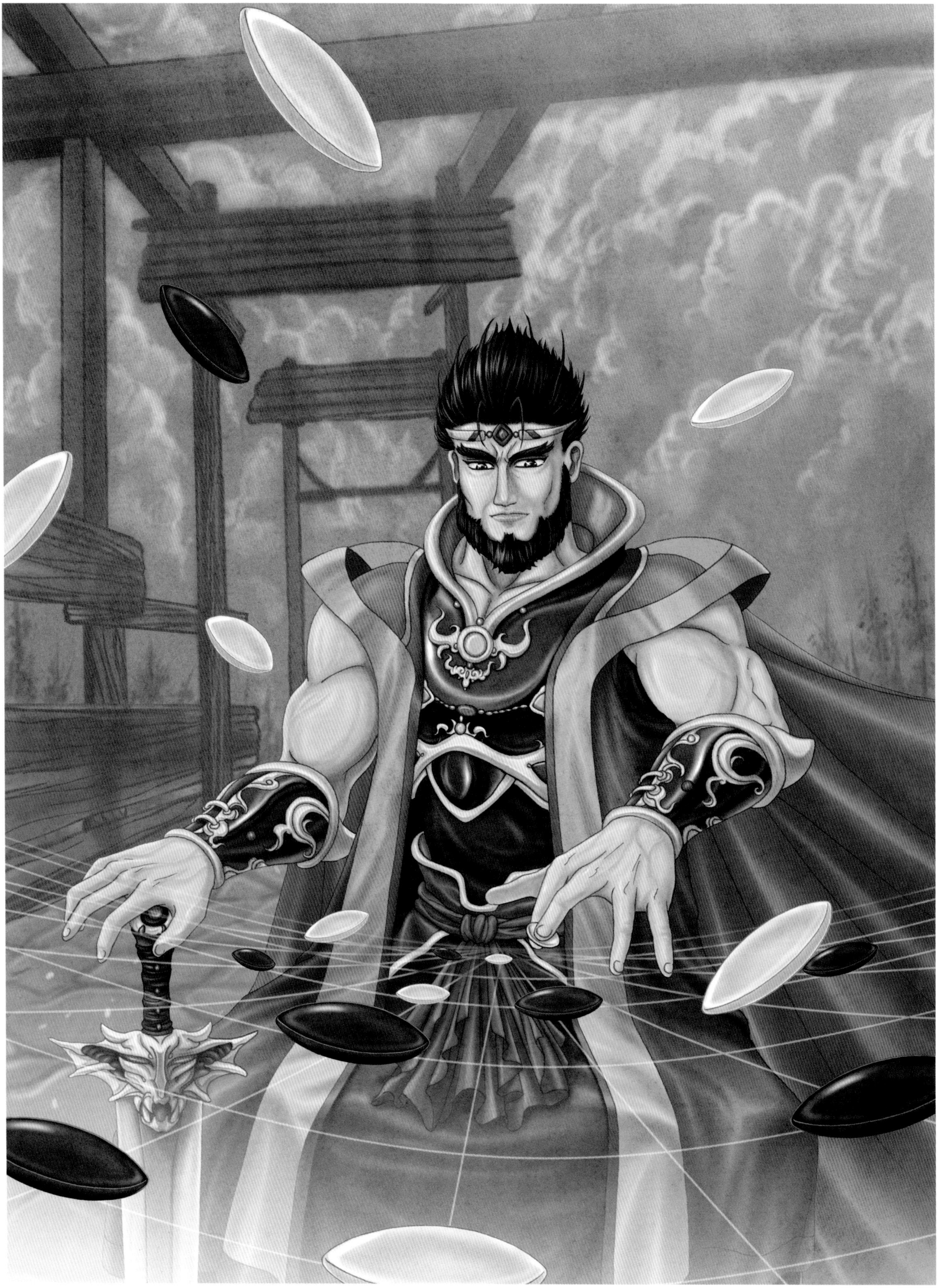

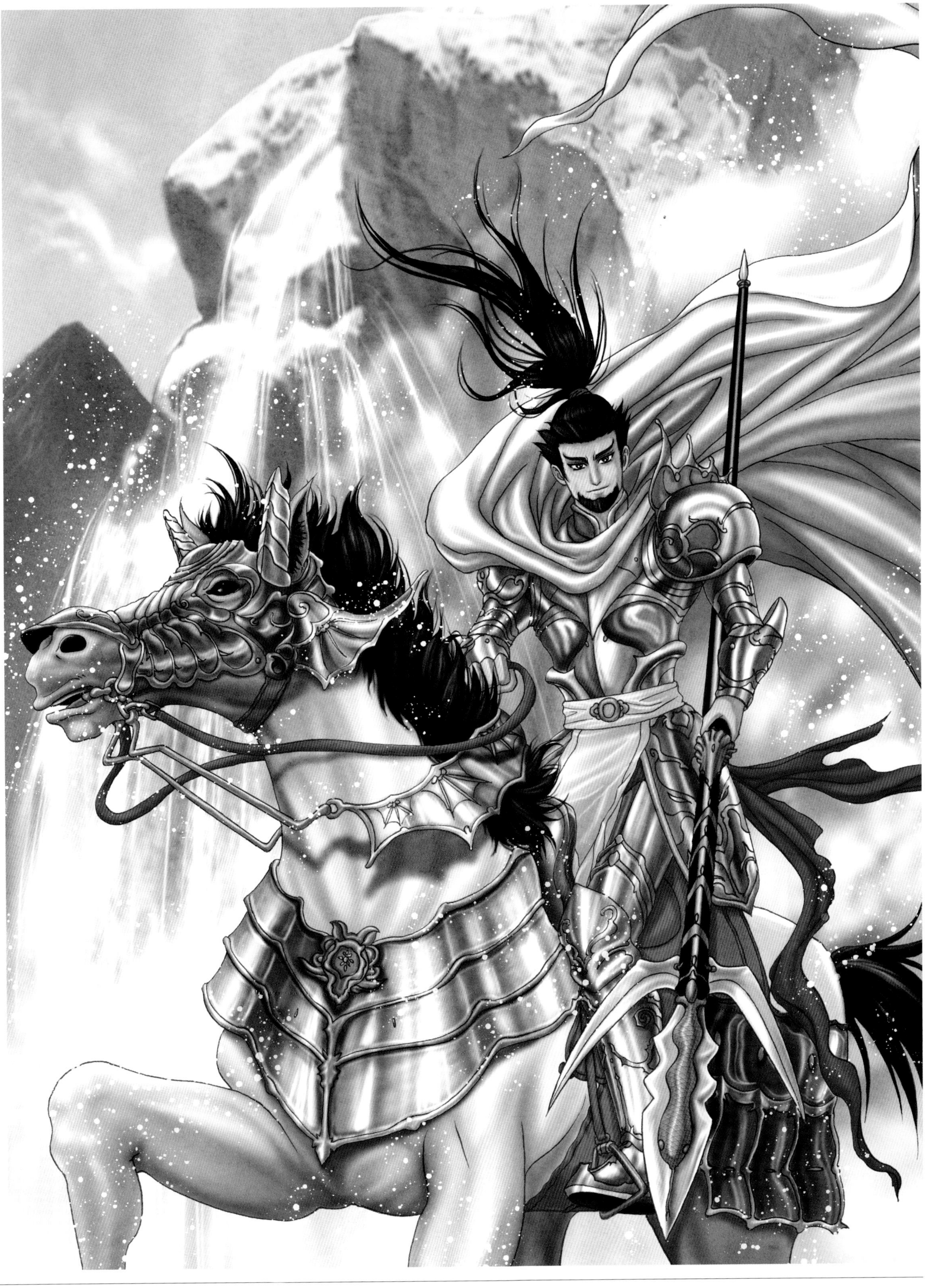

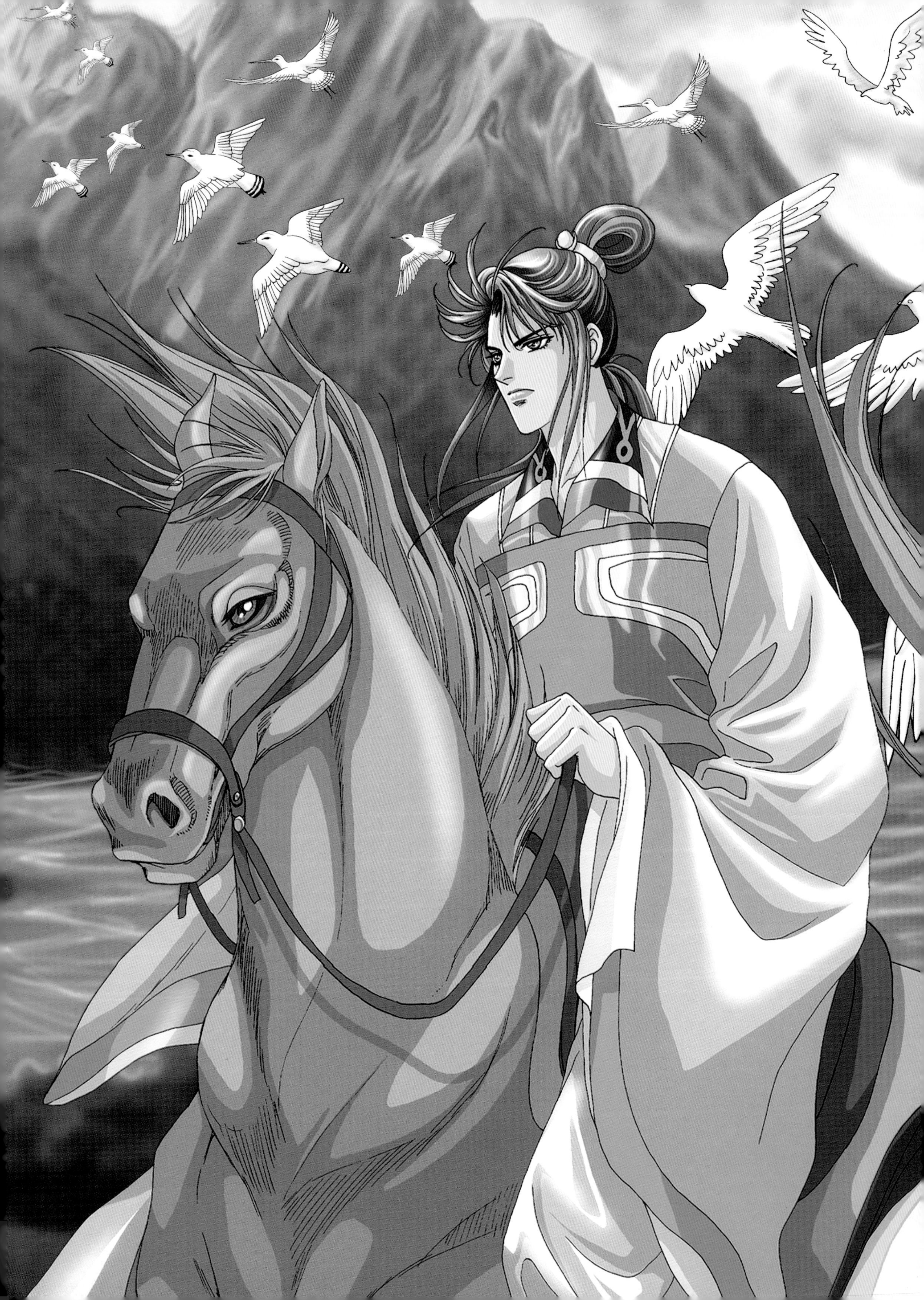

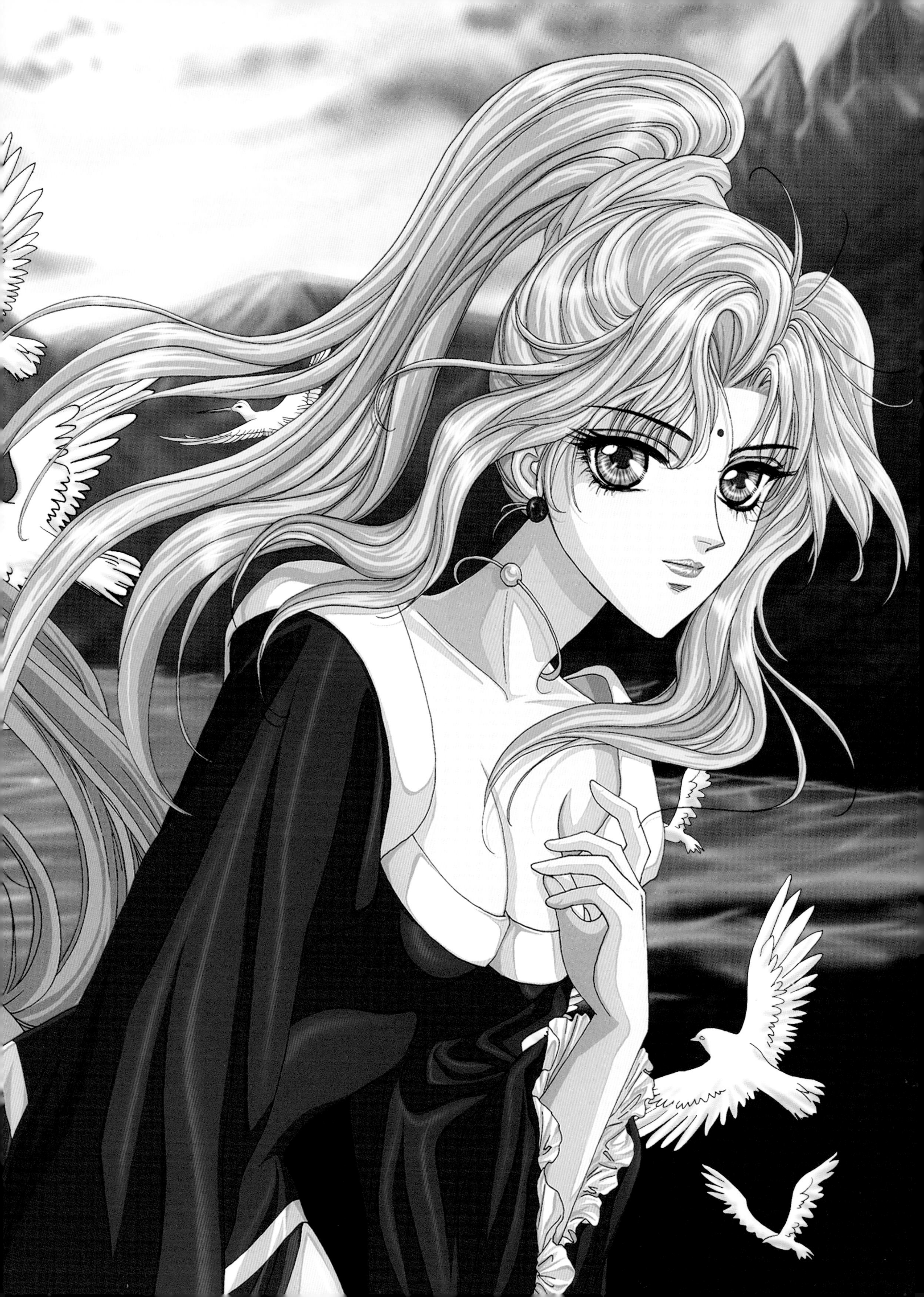

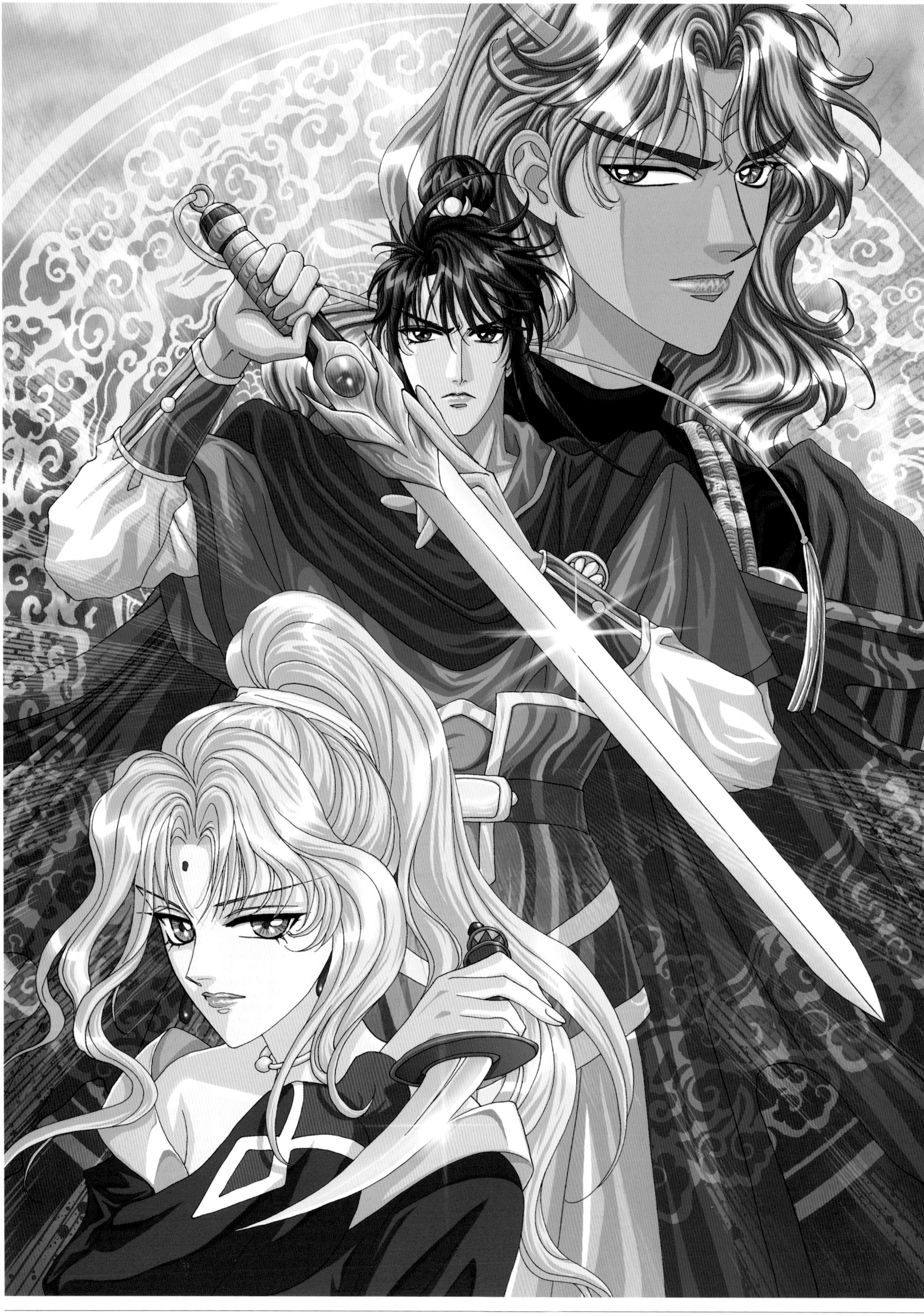

The Artist's **Sketchbook**

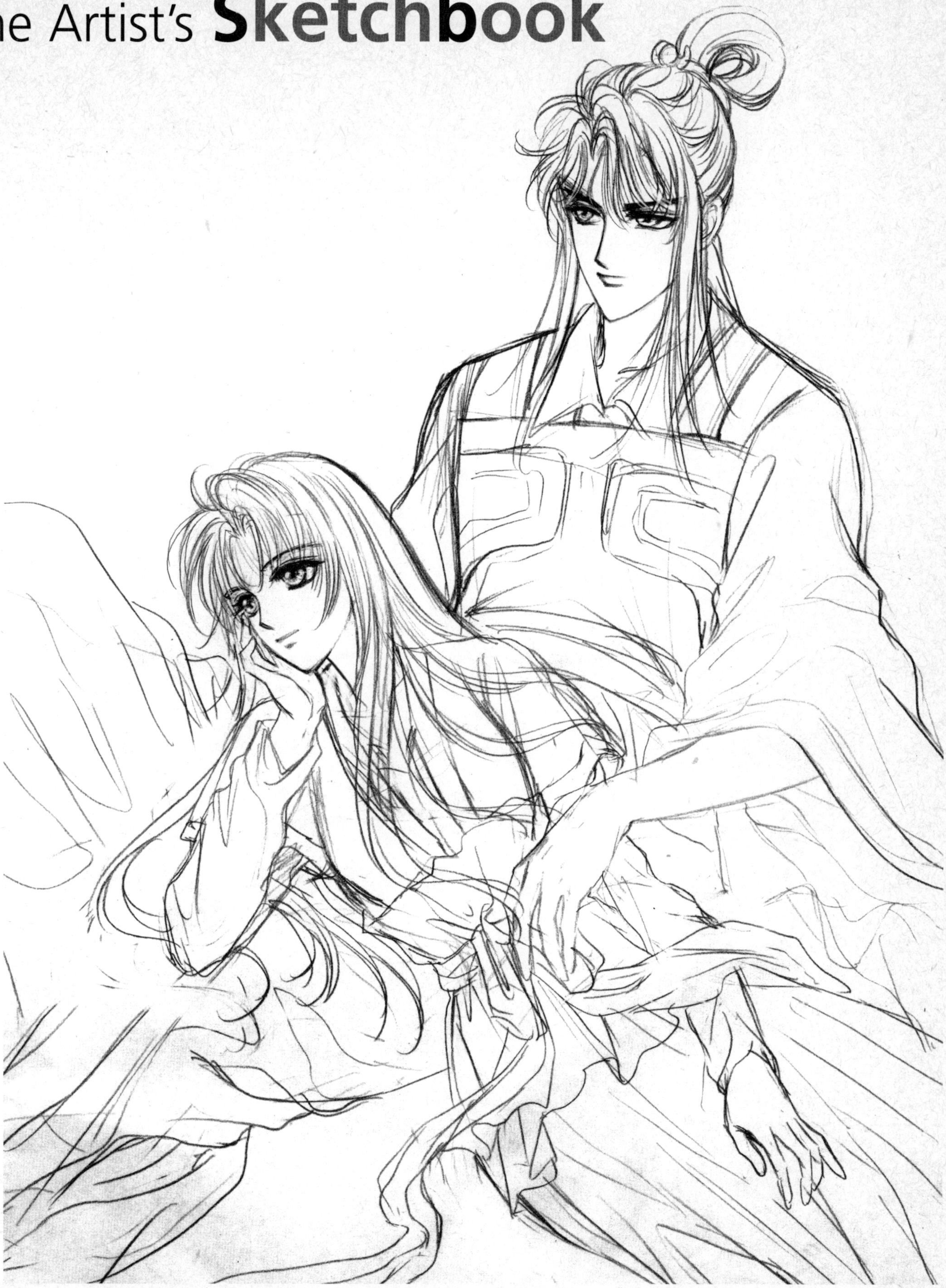

This is a color illustration for the animation original soundtrack of *Sui Tang Ying Xiong Zhuan* (*The Heroes of Sui and Tang*). It is a postcard version, and was distributed as a free gift in the soundtrack package. The character in the illustration is the protagonist, Li Shi Min, with the woman who becomes his wife, Chang Sun Ji. I like drawing characters in ancient Chinese costumes, because the rustling long sleeves and hair is very appealing. (Kao Yung)

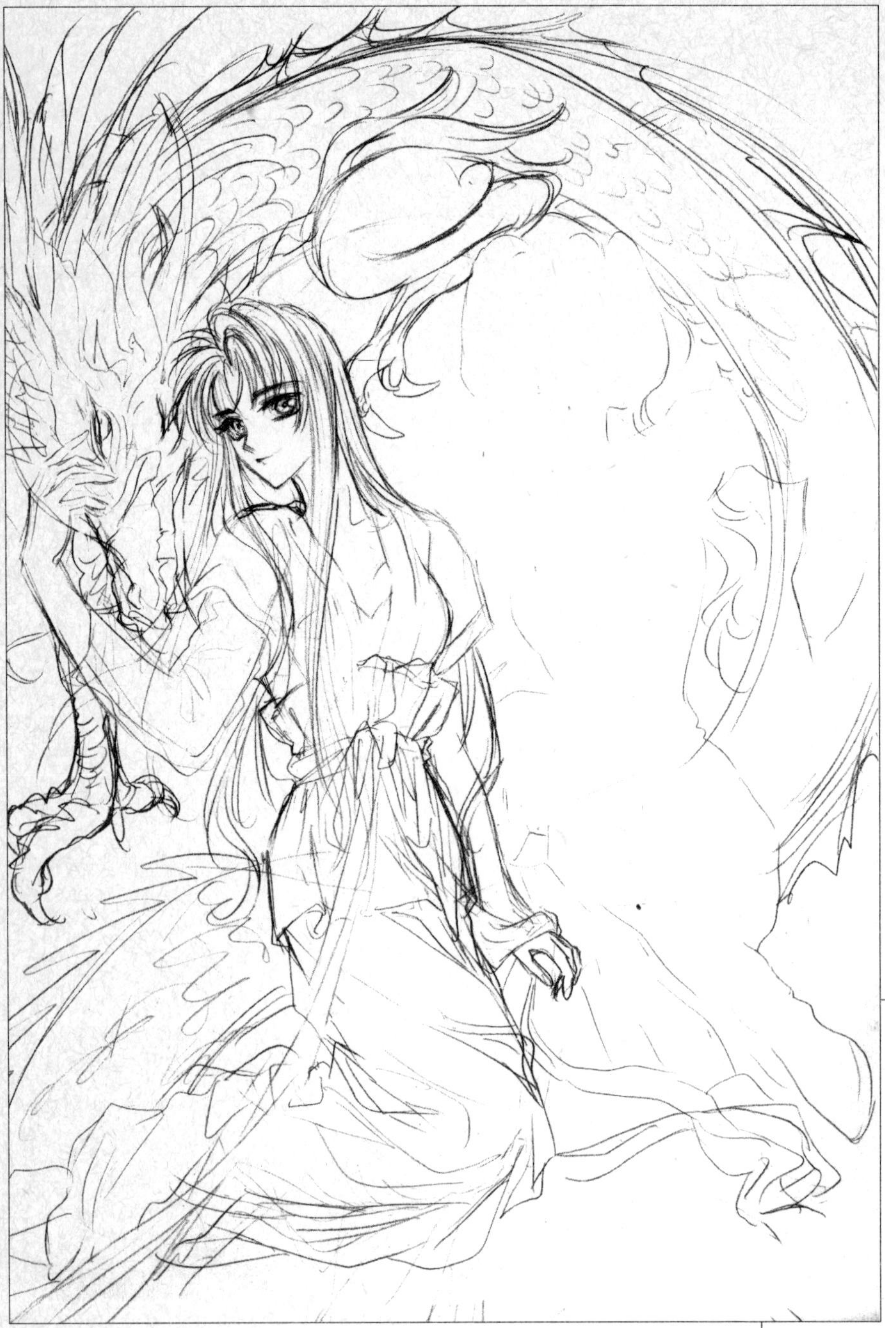

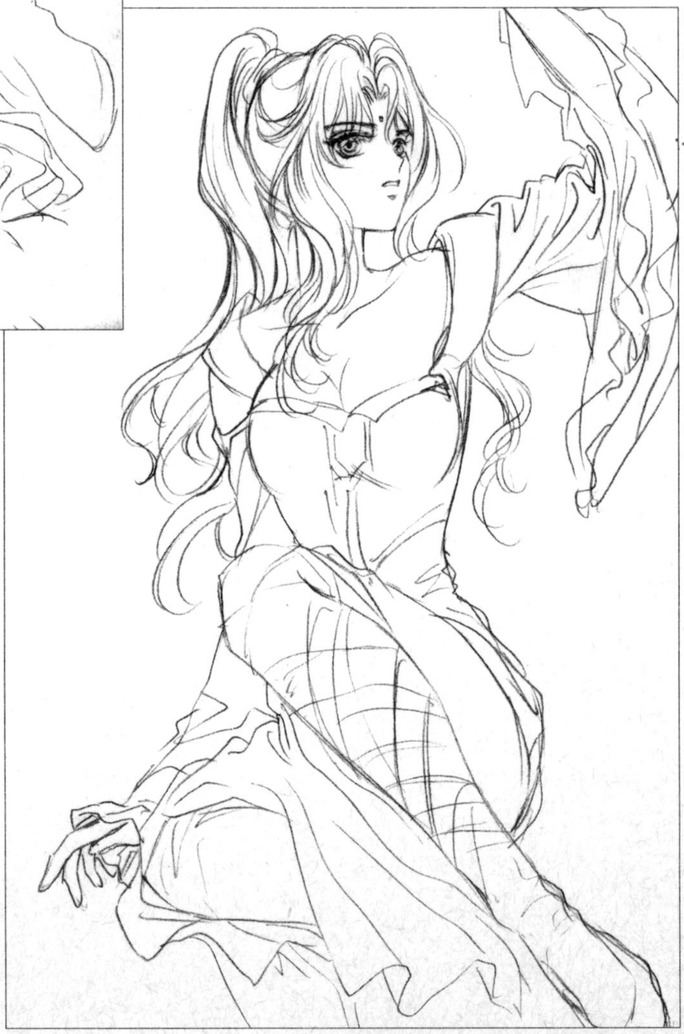

For this sketch, an image came into my mind, and I started with Chang Sun Ji on the left. After that I drew the character on the right, Ge Shu Yun, on another piece of paper, before combining them using a scanner. The character "dragon" also means "emperor" in China, and the fact that Chang Sun Ji and Ge Shu Yun are petting the blue dragon means that this blue dragon is actually Li Shi Min. In other words, it is the later Chinese emperor, Tang Tai Zong. (Kao Yung)

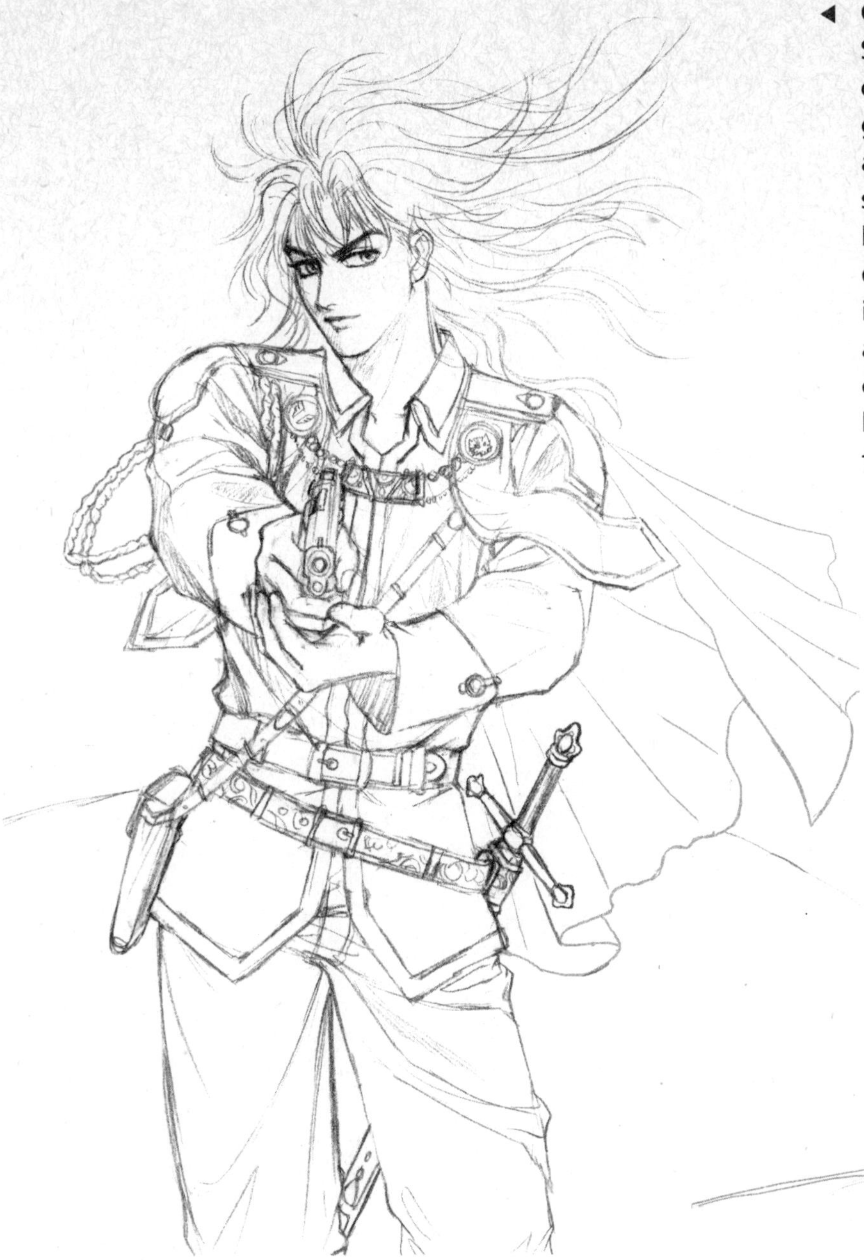

◀ Cover illustration for a different novel series. Since it is a science fiction novel and the main character is a military commander, I drew a young guy in uniform holding a gun. Since black and red are the main color scheme, I thought it lacked something when I had finished, so I added two bullet marks, which gave a good effect. Before drawing this illustration, I was gathering information on military uniforms on the Internet, and I unexpectedly came across at Web page concerning the German military. I was amazed at how perfect it was, and this was an added bonus from doing this illustration. (Kuan-Liang)

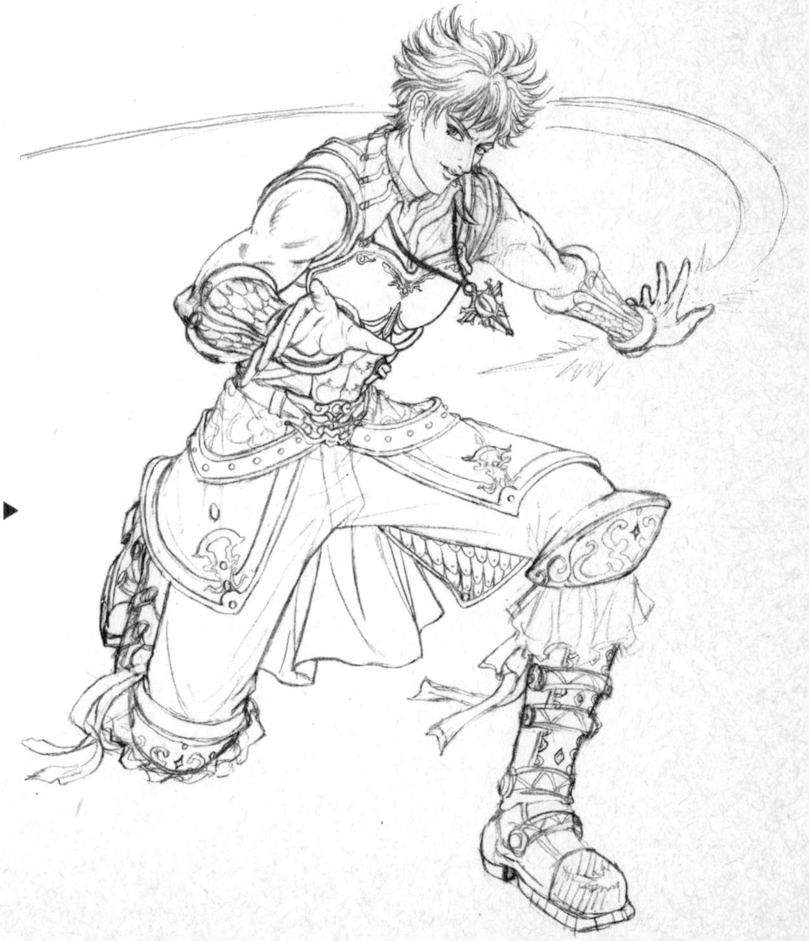

This is a cover illustration for a novel. The story deals with the Western world of magic, and since the main character is a teenager, I drew a wide-eyed youth for the rough sketch. However, the client was not satisfied because what I had drawn did not match the title *Battle of the Gods*. I doubted whether the client understood the content of the novel, so I drew this version to make the youth look more adult. Although I tried my best, the client was still not satisfied. I asked him why, but did not get an answer. Obviously he had not even skimmed through the novel. However, I liked this version a lot, so I finished it as a color illustration. (Kuan-Liang) ▶

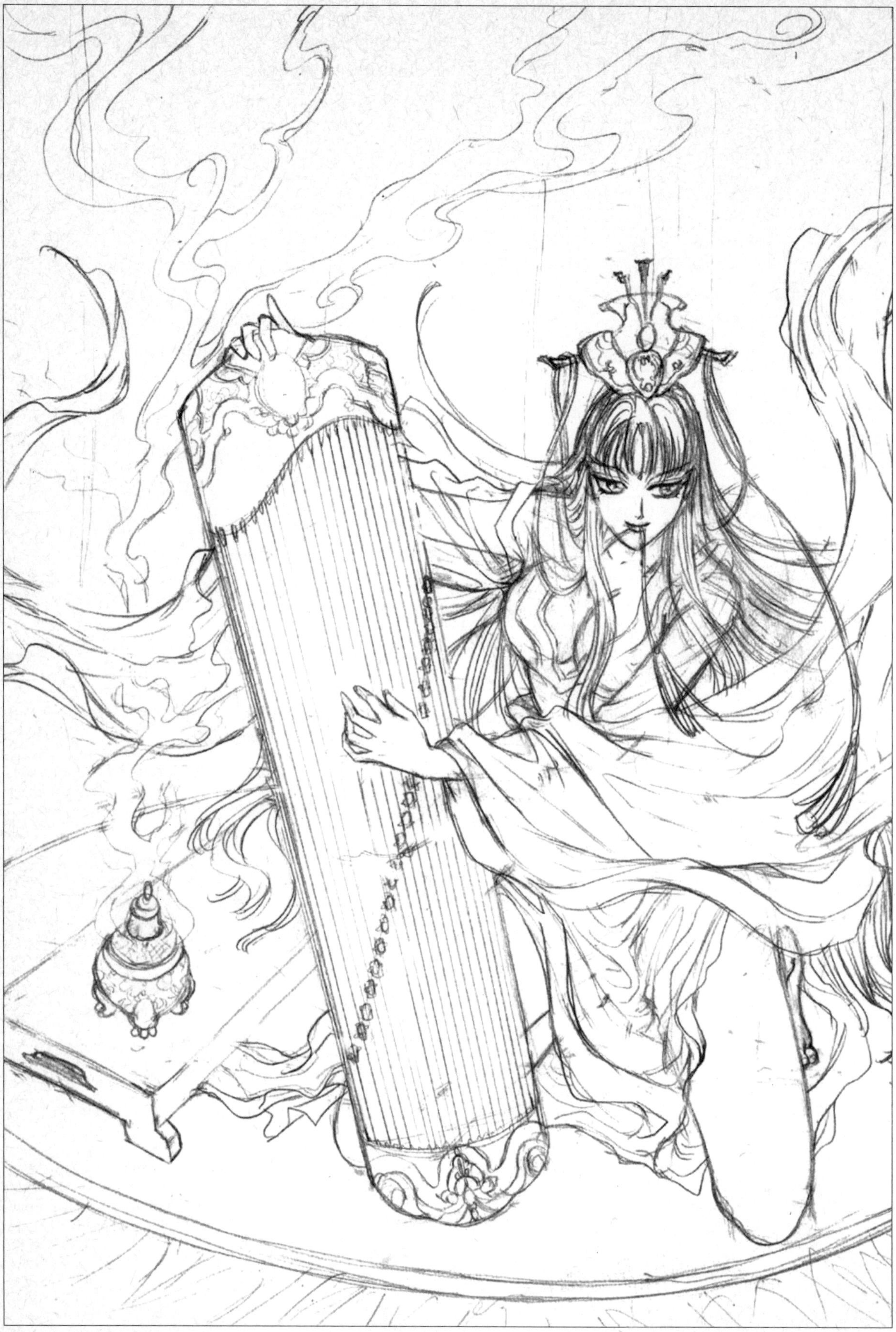

The girl in the illustration is a Chinese *geisha* who has achieved a mastery of the *koto* (Japanese zither). This idea came to mind when I was thinking about the composition. Although the *koto* is usually played while seated, since this did not give the right atmosphere to the illustration, I thought standing and playing the *koto* would better fit the story's image of miraculous talent. The reddish color scheme is also fascinating. I used a lot of techniques in order to create the energetic smoke effect, and I am very satisfied with the way this illustration turned out. (Kuan-Liang)

◀ Originally, I had thought of a hero holding the heroine in his left arm as the composition for this piece. But, that seemed a little trite so I let it go. Anyway, when I pick out a rough sketch for my illustrations, I start by first drawing several different poses. Then I compare them all and choose whichever one turned out the best. Finally, I draw in the lines and fill in the colors. (Kao Yung)

My own color illustration, *Ai Qing Tong Tian Ta* (*Lover's Magic Tower*). Although the man and woman in this piece are both young, it was kind of a challenge for me, as I like to draw adult characters. A manga artist should not stay within boundaries, but should dare to cross them. I drew this manga with that thought in mind. (Kao Yung) ▶

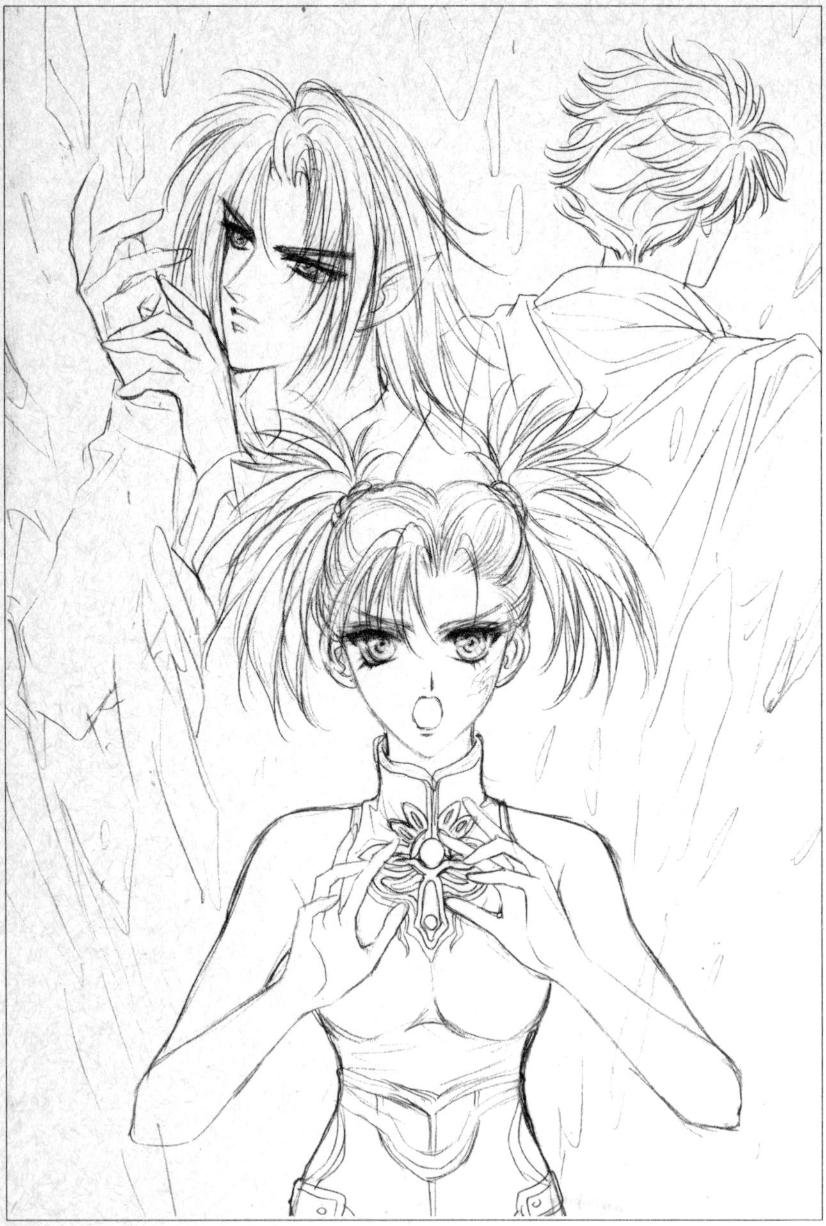

This is a new illustration done especially for the PC game, *The Seven Seal*. The ghosts and spirits of the dead are a favorite subject of mine. The boy with his back turned, with the purple hair, is the one and only Devil. In the game, you only ever see him from behind, and this composition is connected to that. (Kao Yung)

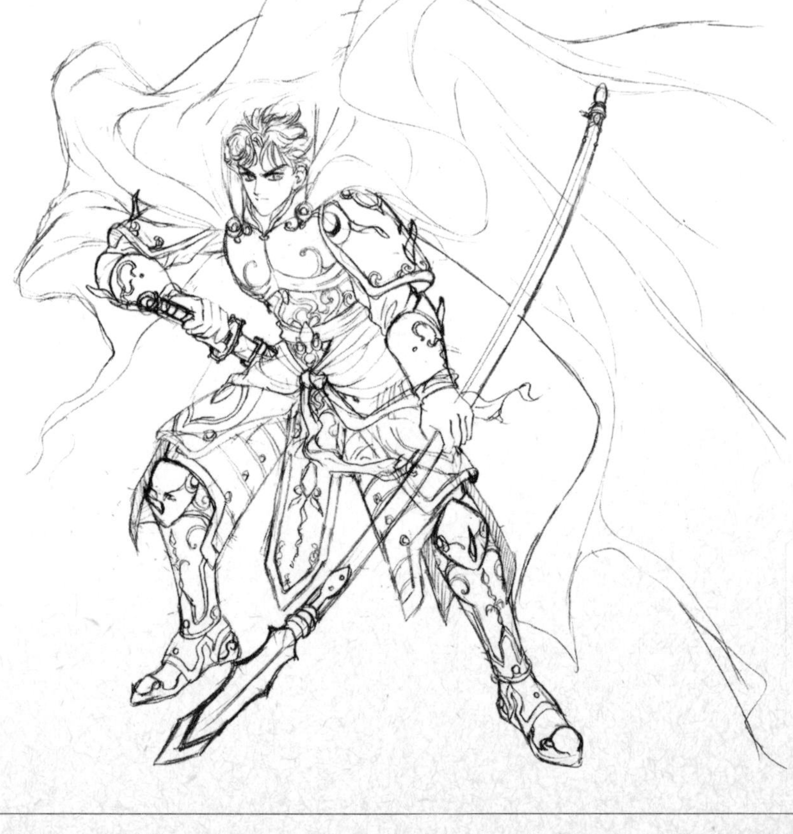

Since this story for this color illustration is set in mythical ancient China, I designed a helm for the main character. I took an old Chinese style helm and gave it a Japanese feel along with Western decorations. Quite a mix, eh? I made the main color indigo, and by drawing in some gilded flowers I was able to give the whole image a feeling of splendor. (Kuan-Liang) ▶

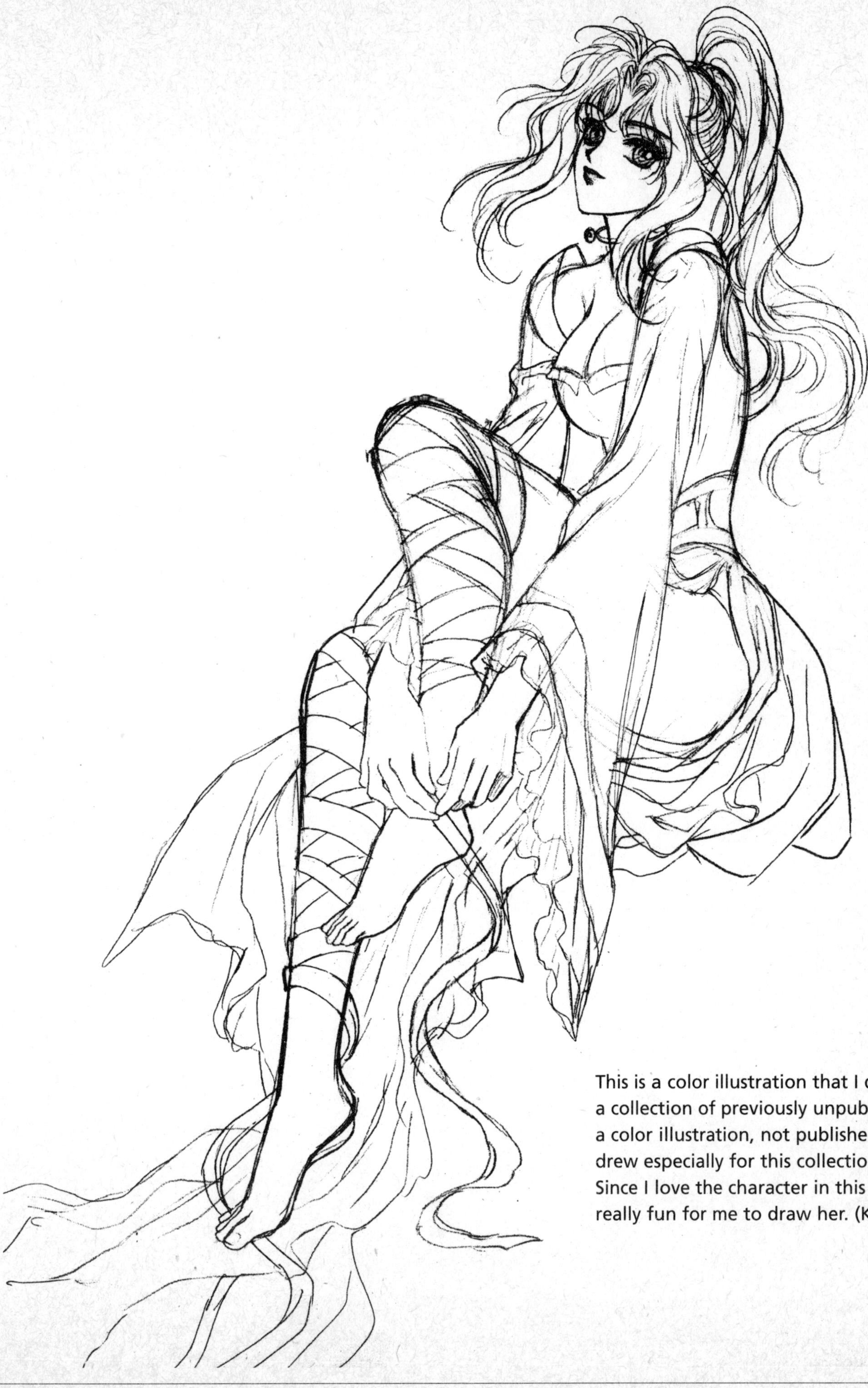

This is a color illustration that I drew especially for a collection of previously unpublished works. This is a color illustration, not published elsewhere, that I drew especially for this collection of illustrations. Since I love the character in this illustration, it is really fun for me to draw her. (Kao Yung)

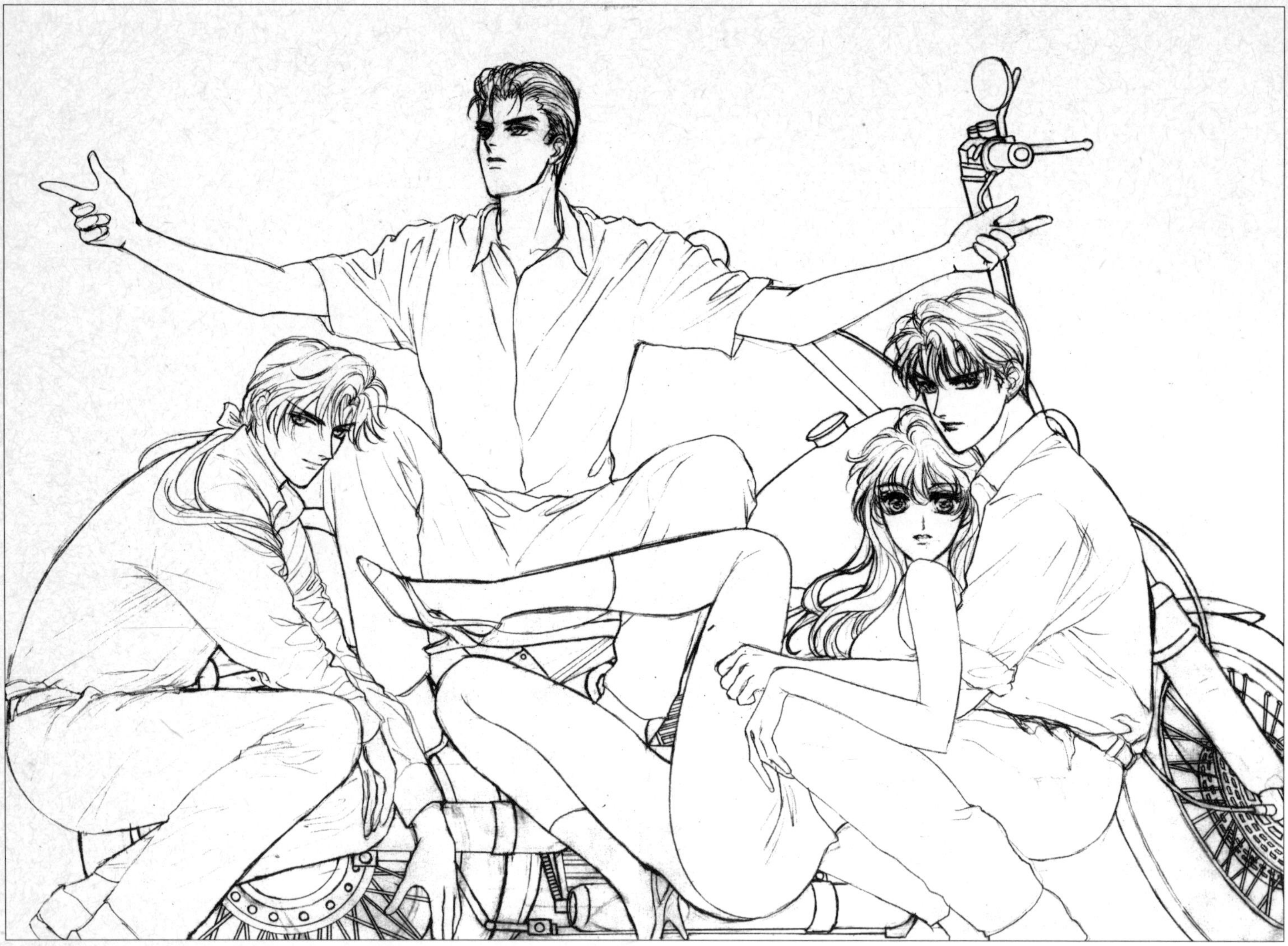

It took quite a lot of time to draw the motorbike in the background, because I'm not very good at drawing mechanical things. But I love drawing people in jeans. (Kao Yung)

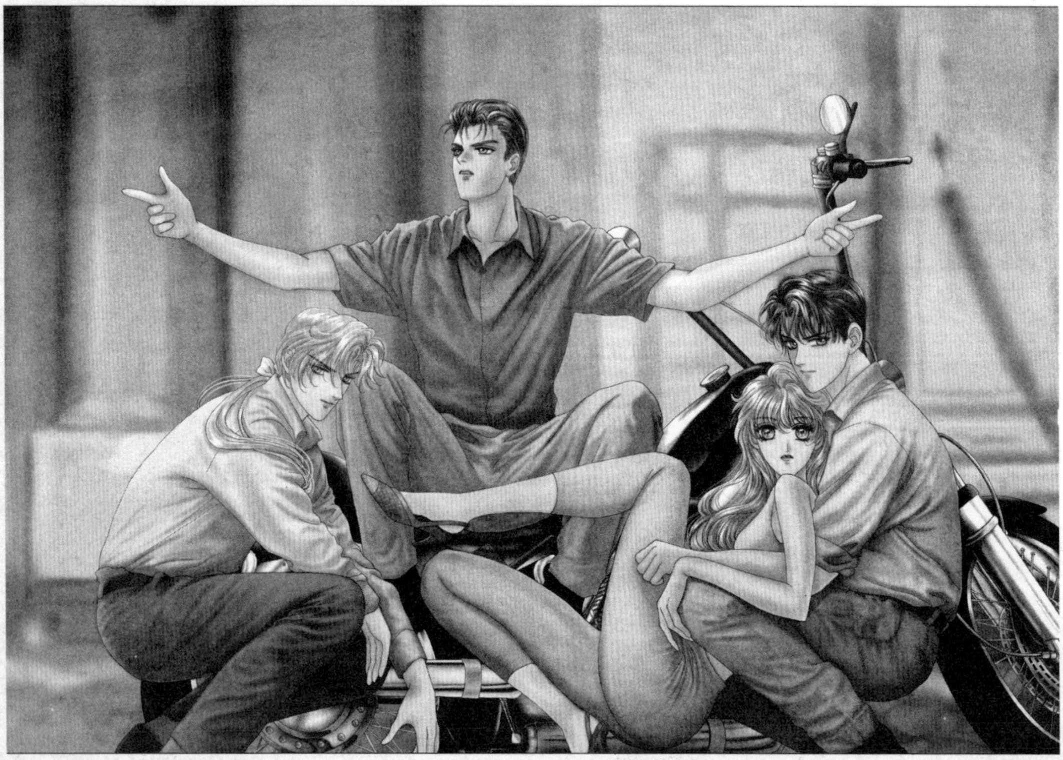

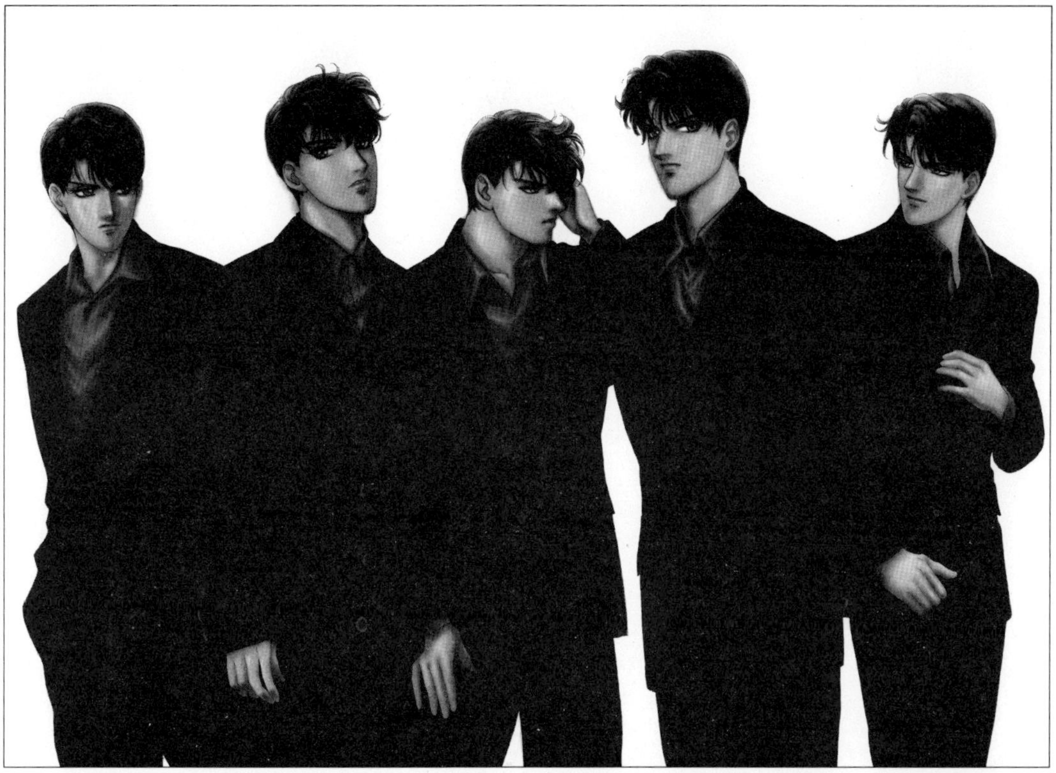

I tried to draw this illustration of attractive young guys wearing suits while using a fashion magazine layout as a reference. What comes out in this picture is that while they are all the same guy, looking at it in this way, the guy looks different depending on an angle. Usually Kuan-Liang handles the coloring of the characters' clothing in all my color illustrations, because he is much better at producing proper fashion pictures. I usually use the blurry watercolor technique for doing clothing. (Kao Yung)

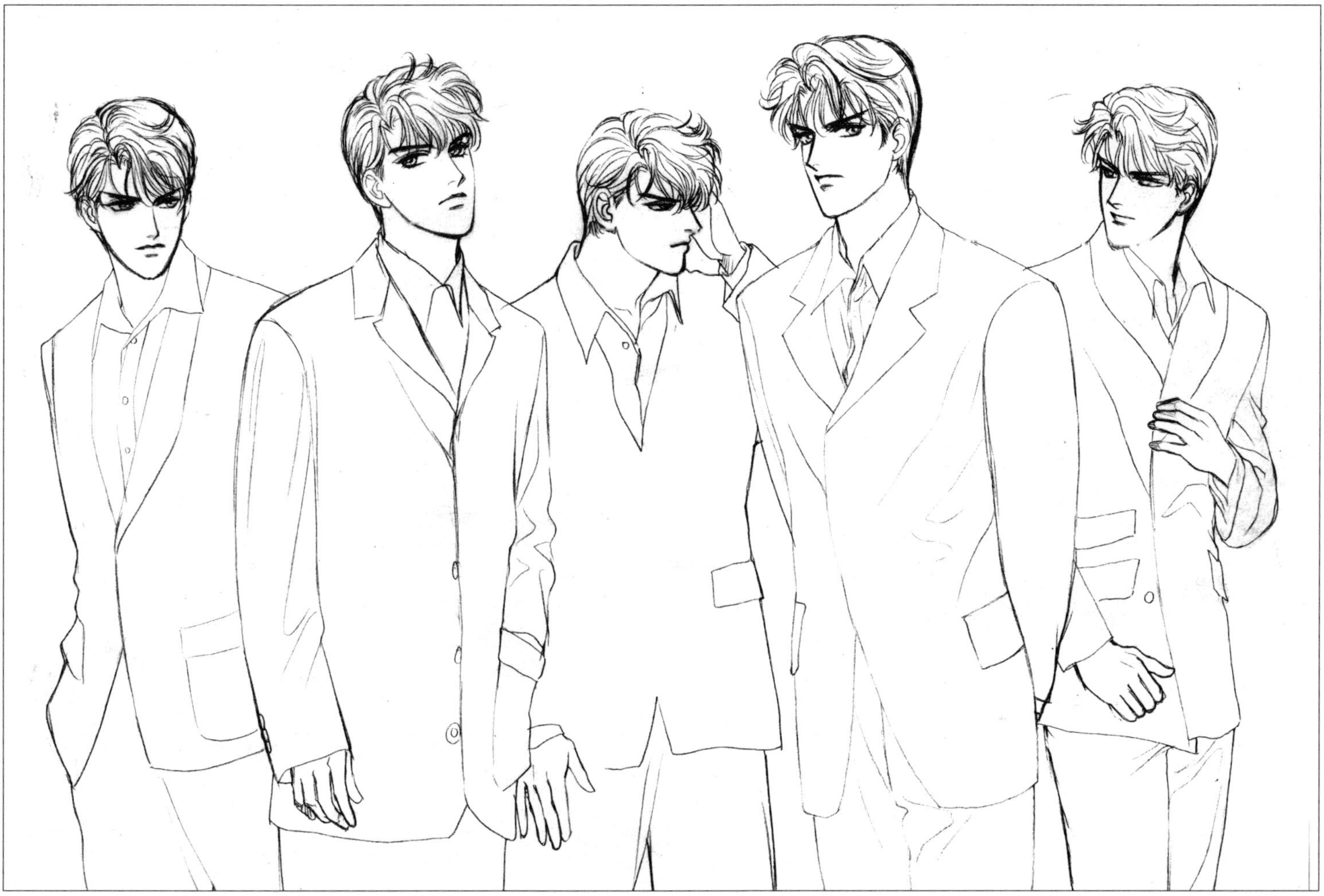

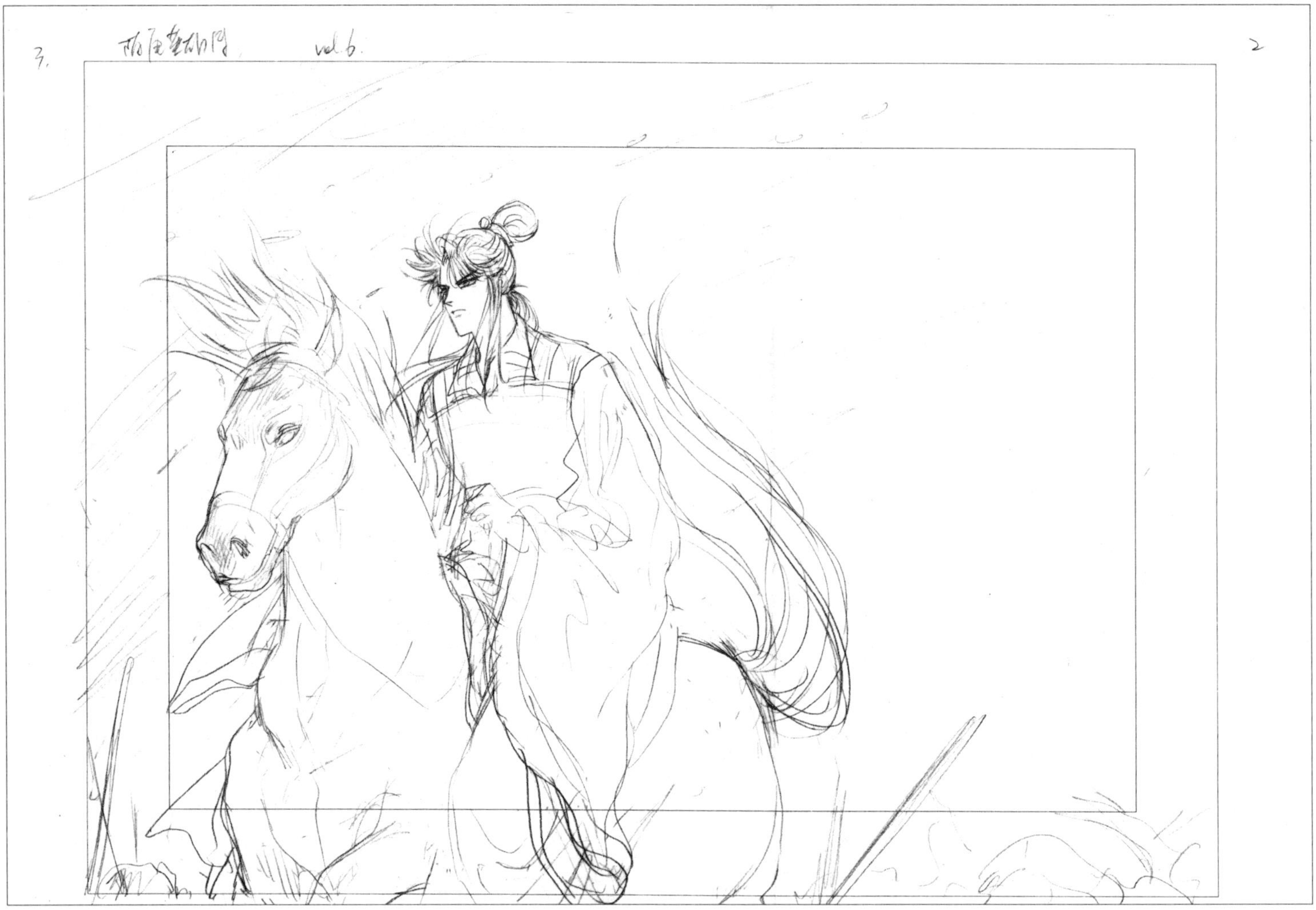

When I work out the concept for a picture, sometimes I use this method. First I draw several character pictures, and then I adjust them until I am satisfied with the combination and size of their arrangement. (Kao Yung)

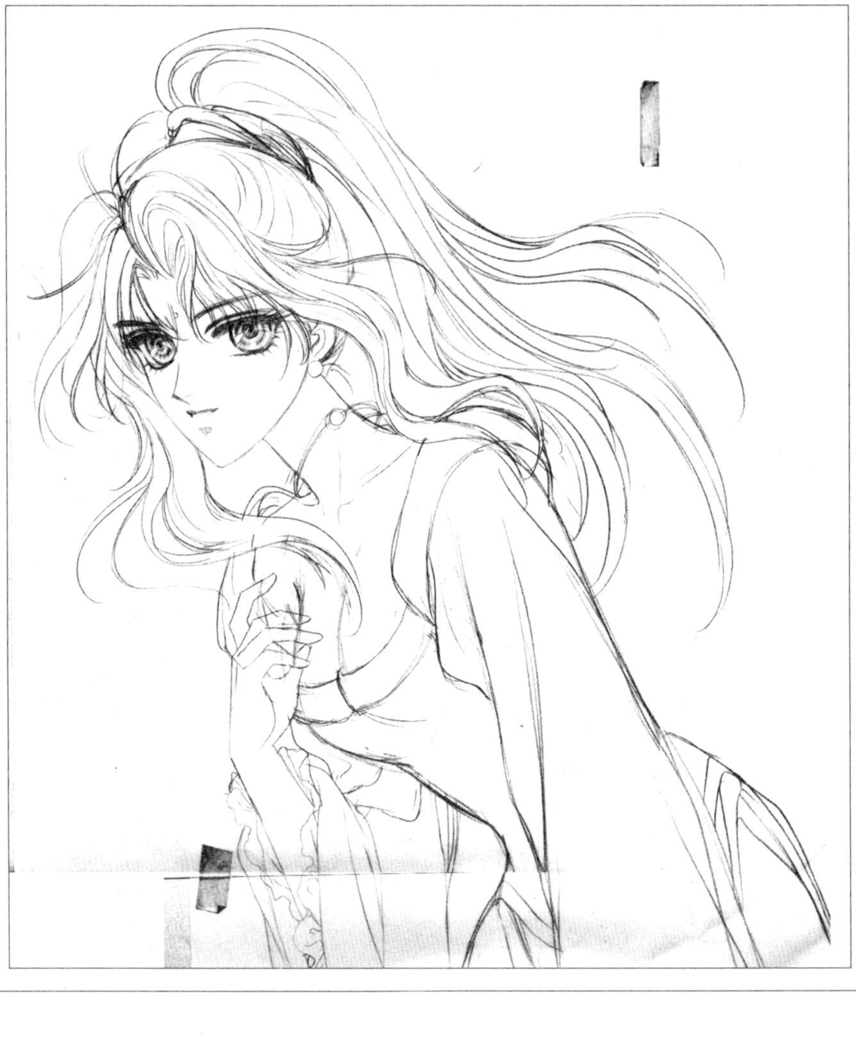

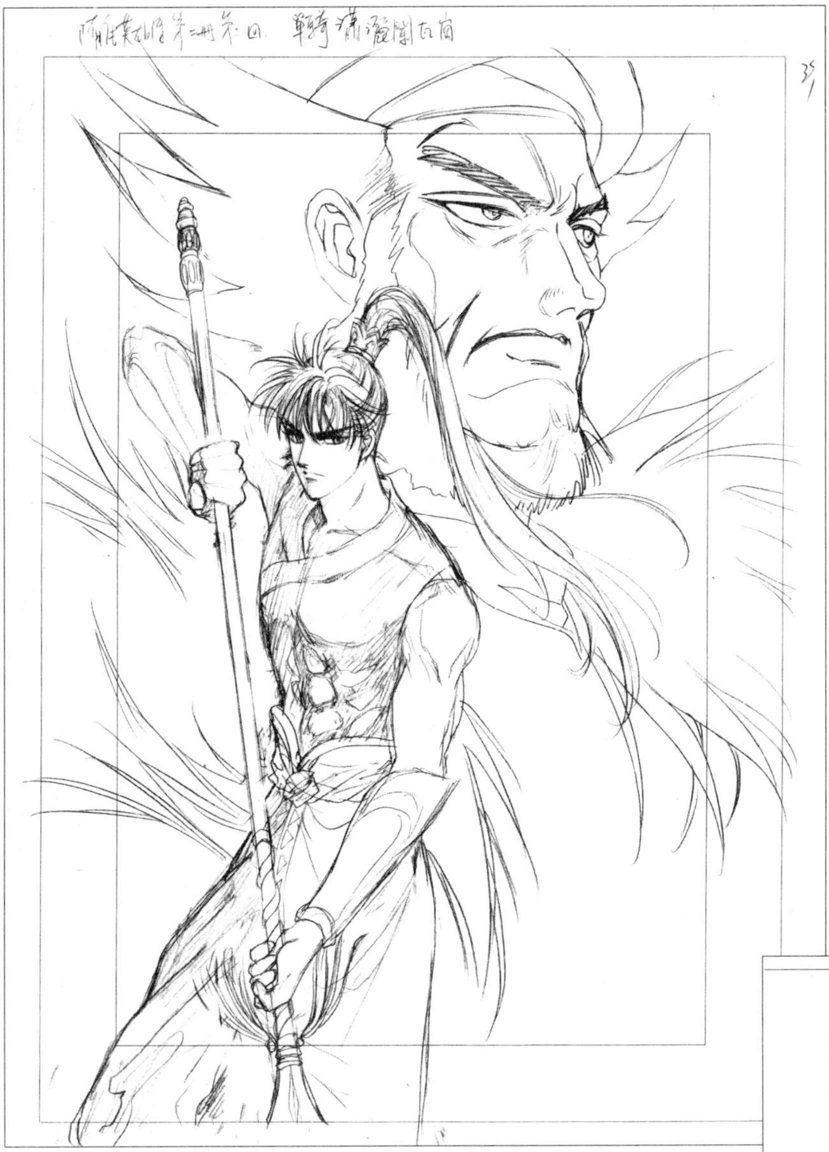

Applying pictures used for manga title pages, I extracted both of the two main characters and combined them in one illustration, which was used for the cover of a separate book. The lightning was created with the PhotoShop filter special effects. (Kao Yung)

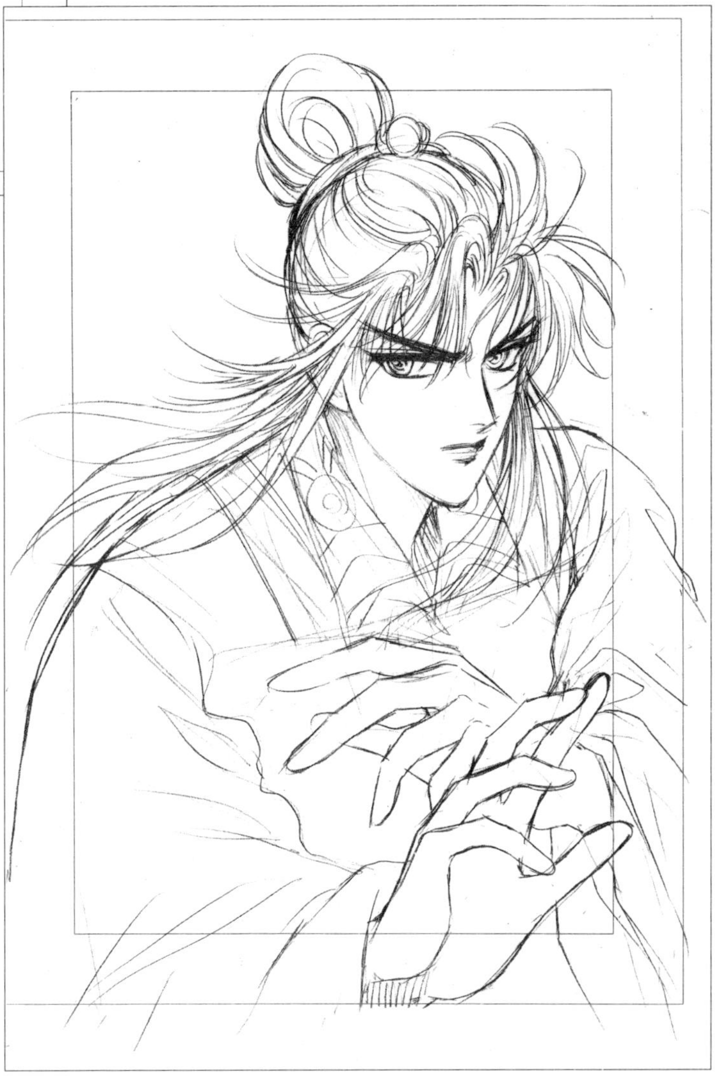

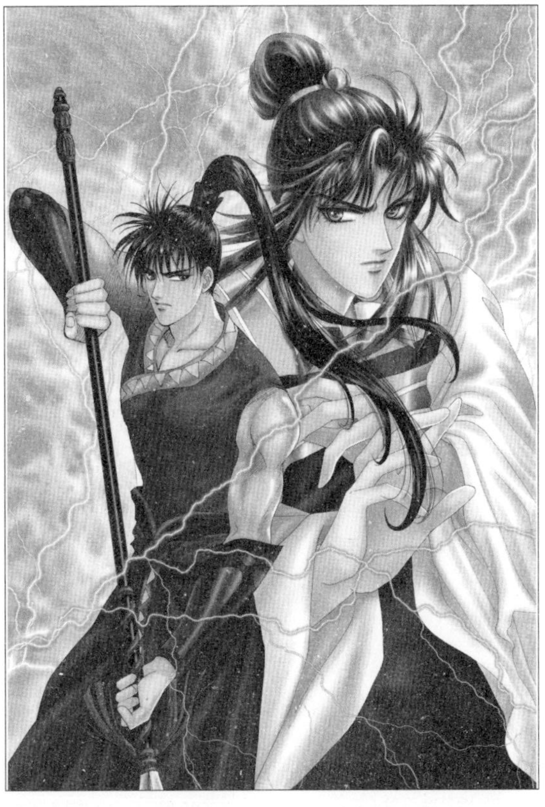

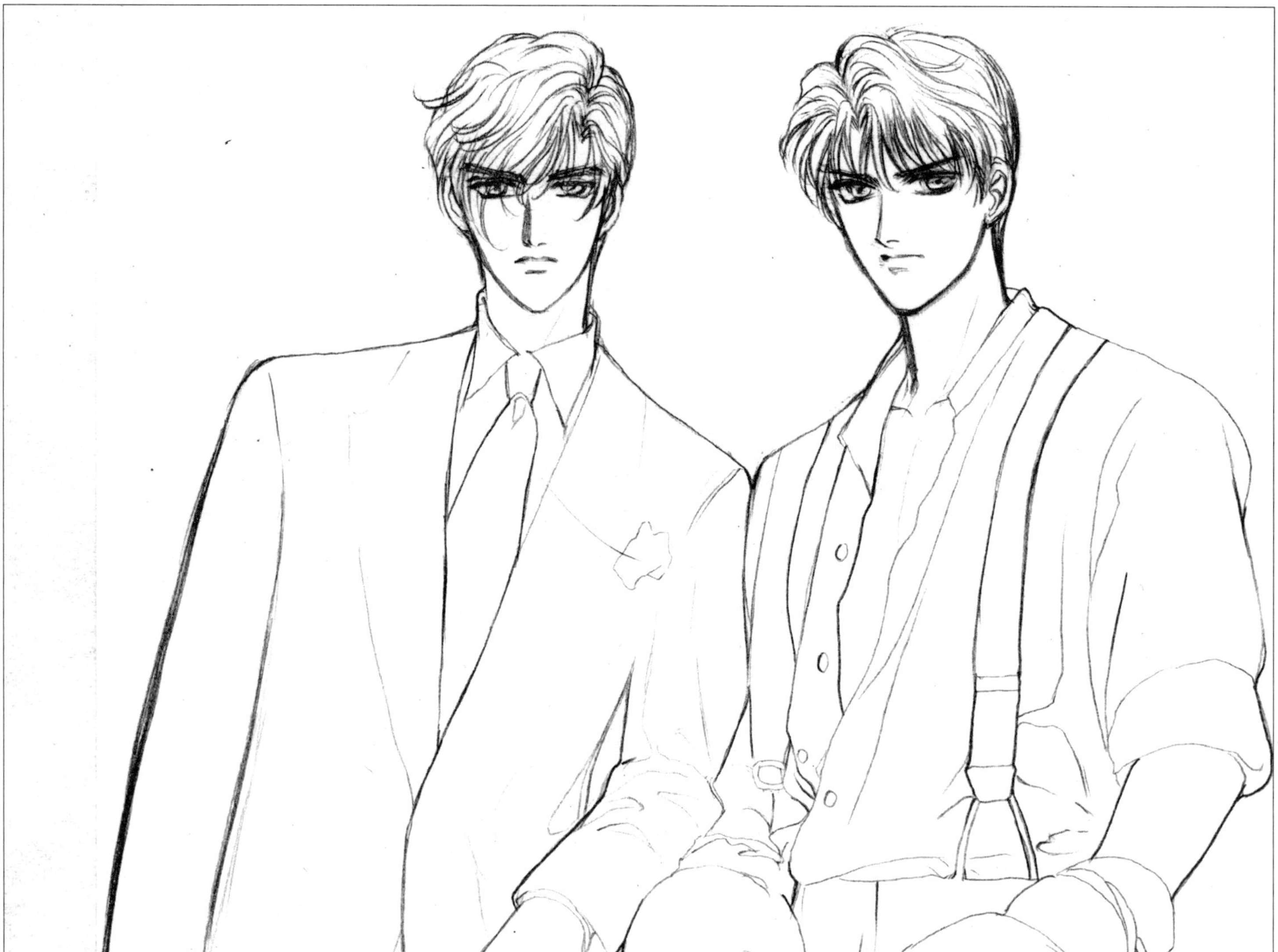

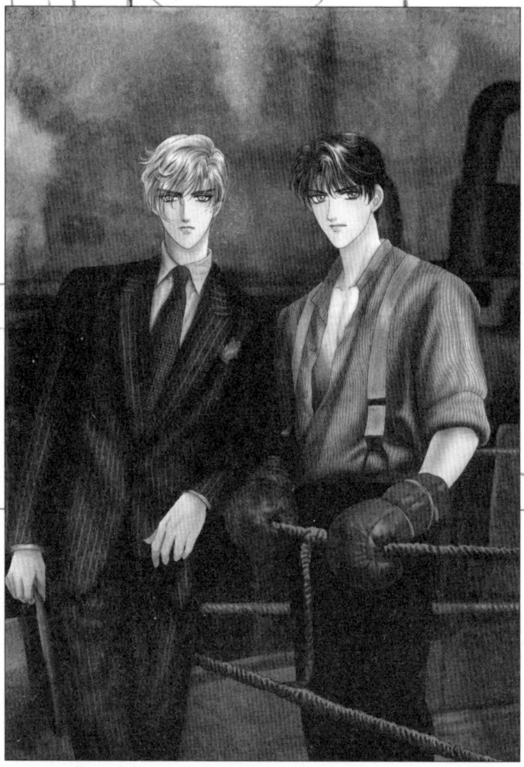

This is a color illustration of the two protagonists of *Heracles*, however from the time that the concept popped into my mind, I decided to render it with a blurred watercolor look using a computer. Using retro sepia colors for the coloring, I consciously tried to evoke the *Godfather* movie in the clothing. This is because I personally love the atmosphere of New York mafia movies. (Kao Yung)

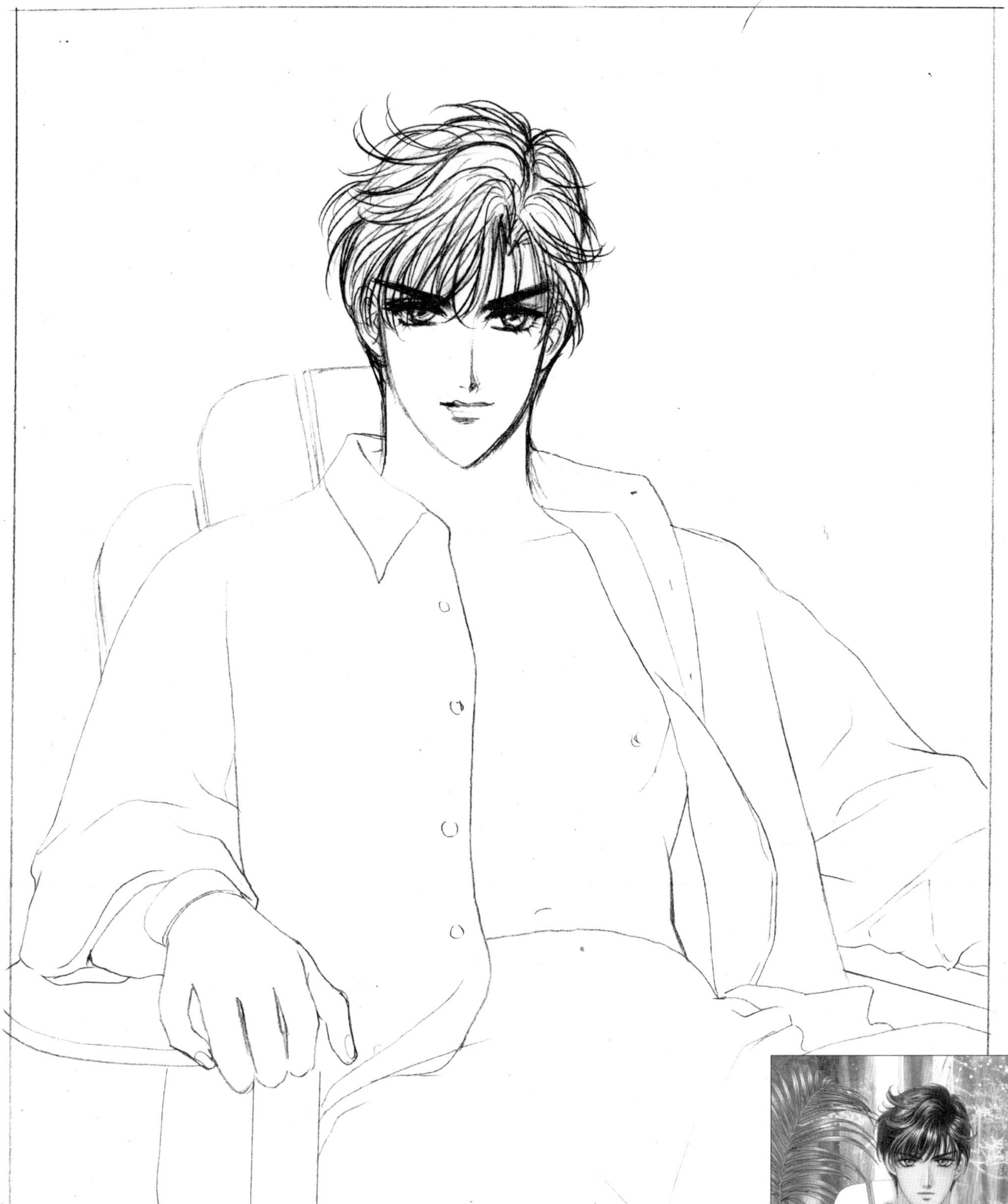

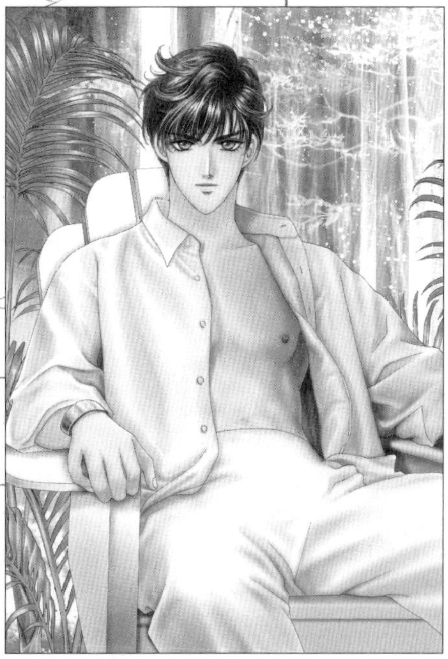

This is a color illustration used in an explanation of how to use PhotoShop, in the Taiwanese magazine, *HOT CG*. I like fusing computer and hand drawn colors, because it gives it a natural touch. The waterfall in the background was completed based on this idea. (Kao Yung)

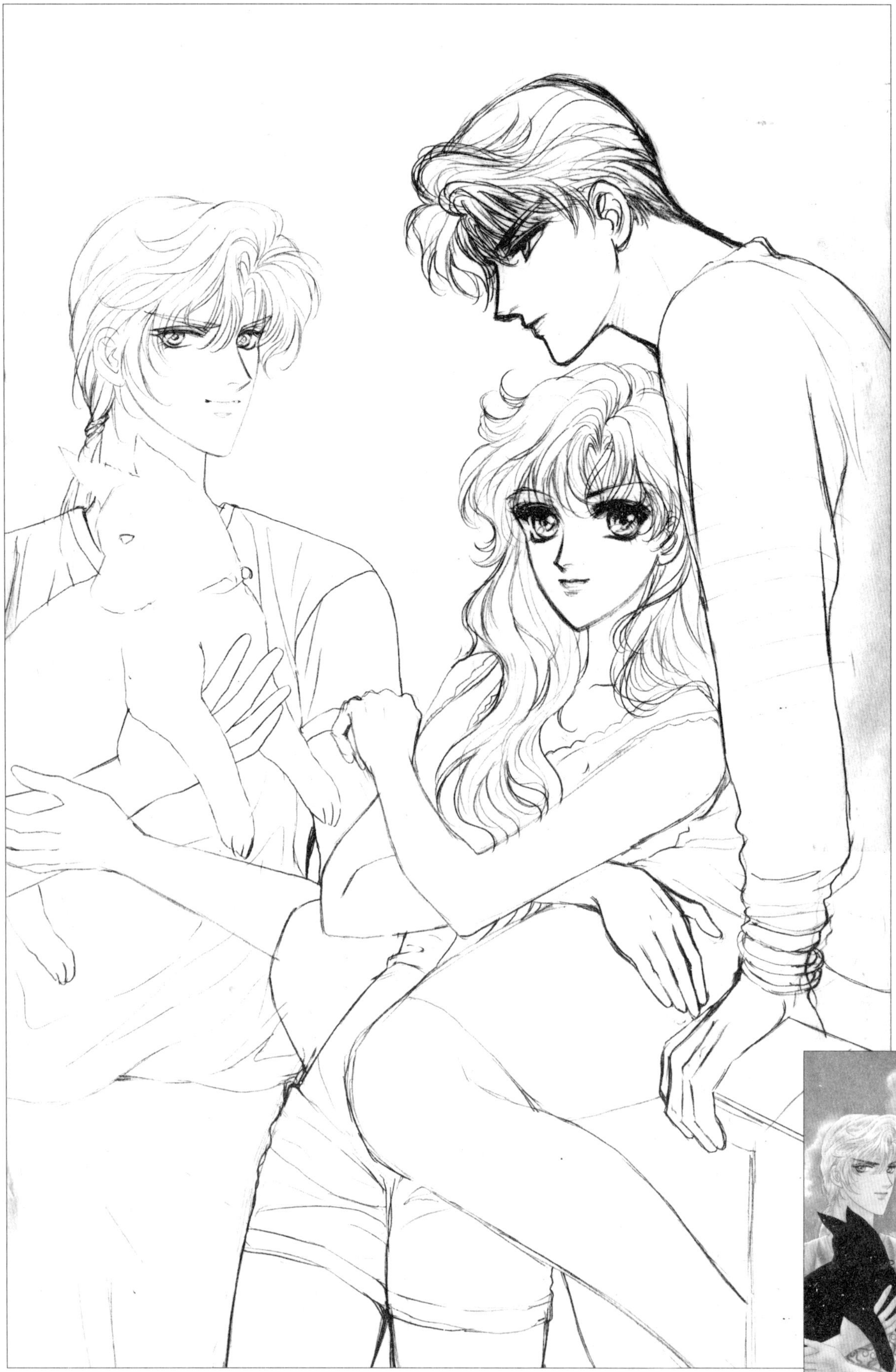

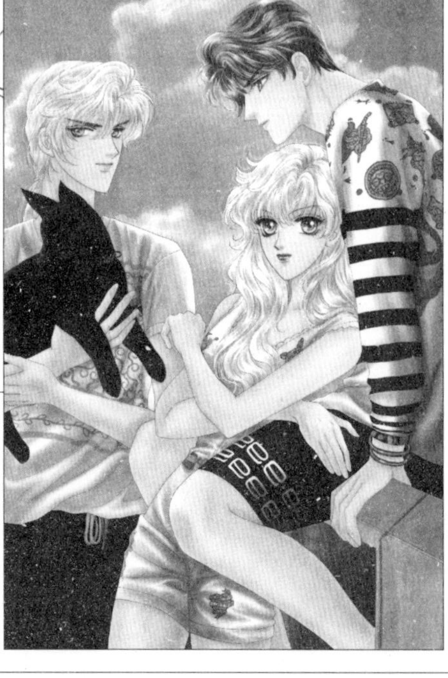

This is a work published in the Taiwanese edition of a collection of reproduced originals called *Heracles*. Since I love to use the computer to create the atmosphere of a hand drawn illustration, if you look closely you can find a clear paper design in various parts. When I am not busy with work, I go to the suburbs with a relaxed feeling like I drew in this illustration. The feeling when you see white clouds in a blue sky is really great. (Kao Yung)

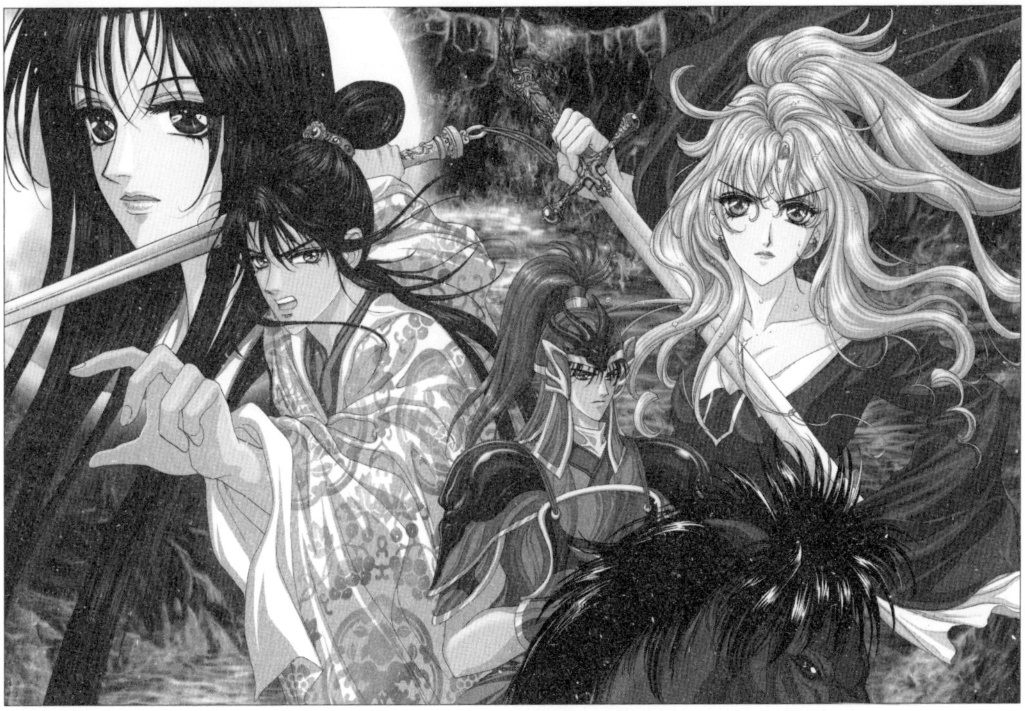

This work was completed for the title page of the first volume of *Sui Tang Ying Xiong Zhuan* (*The Heroes of Sui and Tang*) manga edition. I did the basic lines, and Kuan-Liang finished the other coloring. (Kao Yung)

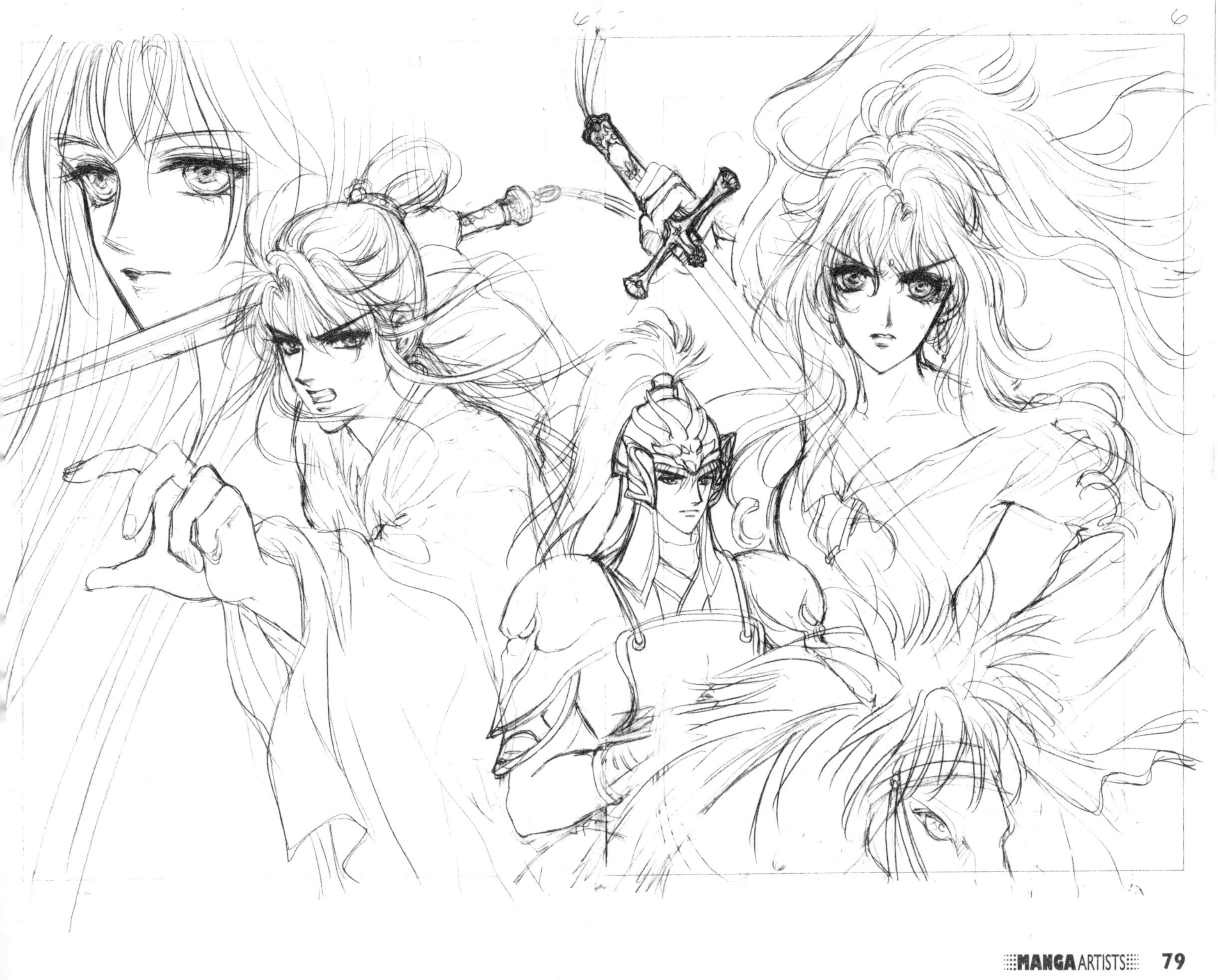

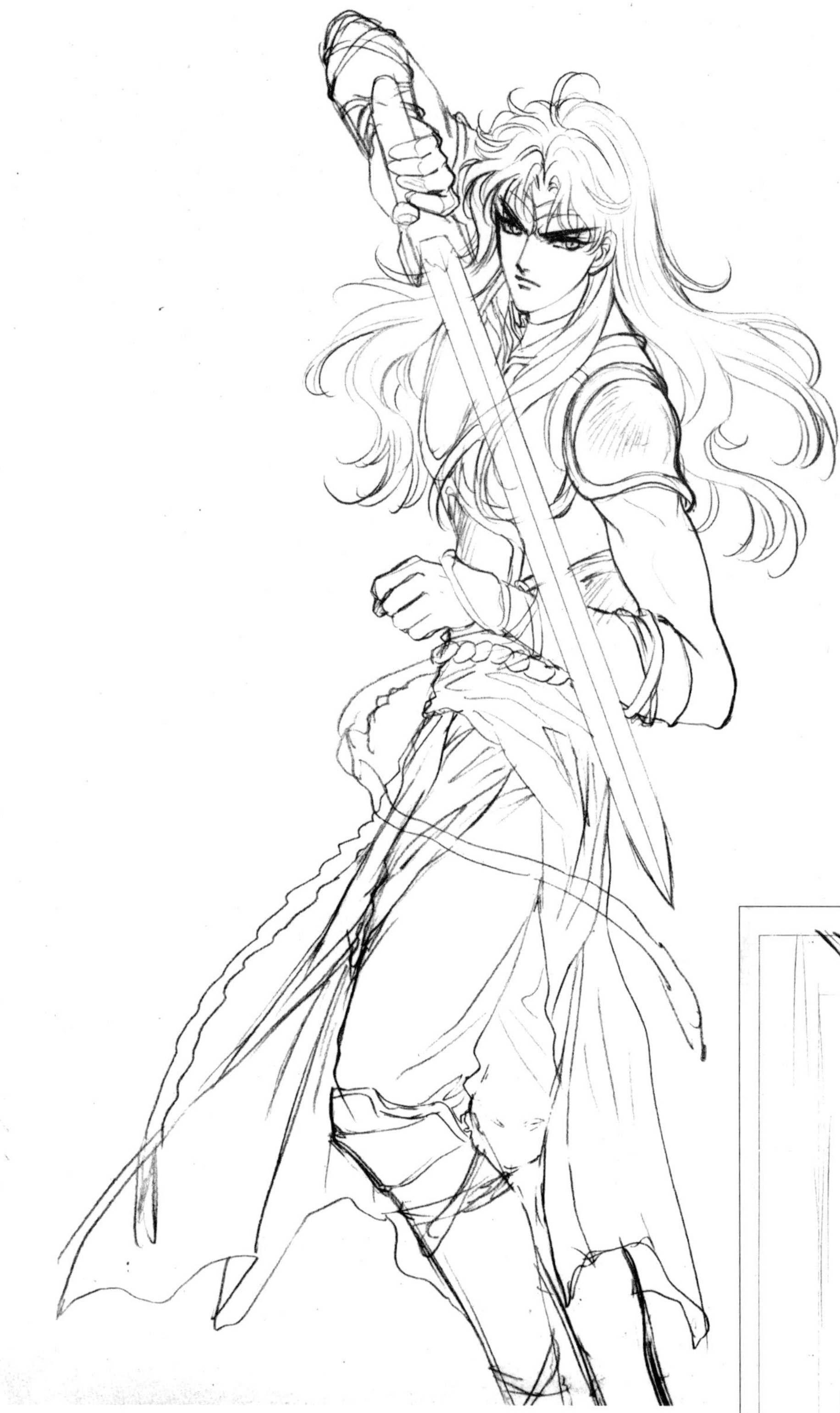

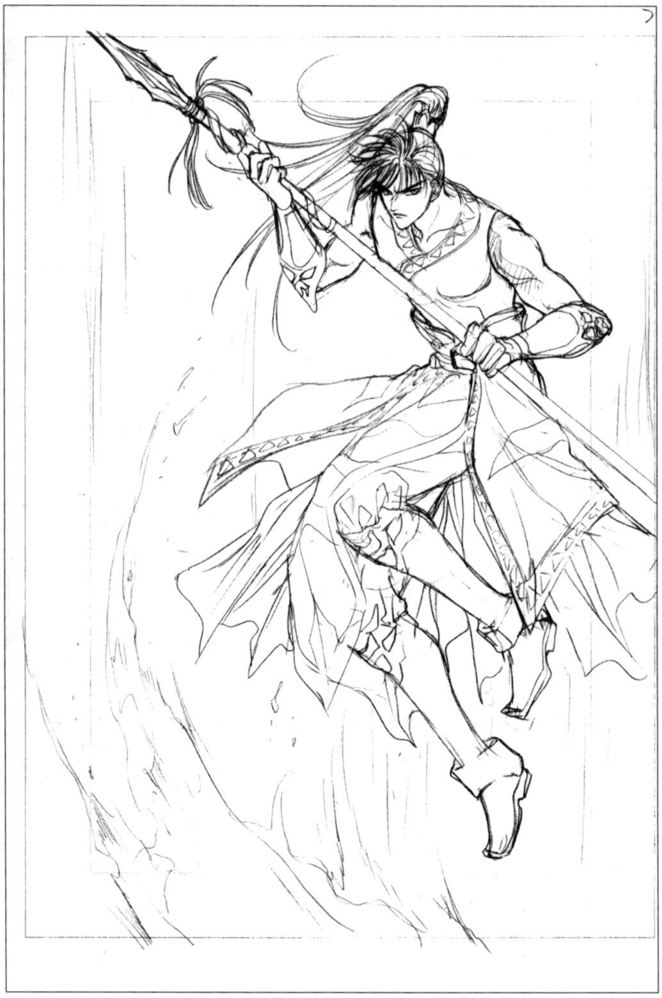

At the request of the director of *Sui Tang Ying Xiong Zhuan* (*The Heroes of Sui and Tang*), an animated film made in conjunction with Shanghai Animation Film Studio, this is an illustration I drew of six characters on a scroll-like sheet. The director intended to use the illustration as a background for the ending sequence of the film. Since it is seldom that I draw such a long horizontal work, it was extremely difficult to do. (Kao Yung)

Profile of Kao Yung & Kuan-Lian

Kao Yung

■ Date of Birth: July 3rd, 1966
Birthplace: Taiwan R.O.C.
Hobbies: Reading, Listening to Music, Writing Novels,
                Playing with Dogs
Education: National Chengchi University, Department of Law

Kao's works are published in many languages and have been translated in Taiwan, Mainland China, Japan, South Korea, Indonesia, and Thailand.

His works are hailed as elegant and fantastic. His stories are extremely detailed and yet posses both depth and charm. People call him, "The Godfather of Beauty."

■ **Works**
Brahma-Upanishad Vol. 1—3 / Heracles Vol. 1—12 /
Calendar 1996—Dream / The Love Season Vol. 1—3 /
Original Sin Illustration */ The Passion Tarot Deck,*
The Kao Yung Tarot Deck / Hopefully Astrology—The Love /
Hopefully Astrology—The Romance / What's Happy / Juliet Sadness /
Diana: Queen of The True Heart / Calendar 2000—Heracles /
Heracles Original Illustrations */ Lover's Magic Tower Vol. 1—2*

July	1994	*Brahma-Upanishad*, Korean language series begins in the Korean magazine *Color*. *Brahma-Upanishad*, Japanese language edition is published by MOVIC, Inc.
April	1995	*The Love Season*, Chinese language edition is published by Daran Publishing Company Ltd. *Michelle in the Wild West*, Japanese language edition is published by Jitsugyo no Nihon Sha Ltd.
January	1997	*Original Sin*: *Collection of Images* is published by Daran Publishing Company, Ltd.
August	1997	*The Passion Tarot Deck* goes on sale.
November	1998	*The Heracles series* continues with Ever Glory Publishing Company Ltd.
October	1999	2000 Calendar—*Heracles* Participates in the 3rd Asian Manga Summit and original illustration exhibition held by the Asian Manga Summit Committee.
August	2000	Participates in the 4th Asian Manga Summit and original illustration exhibition held by the Asian Manga Summit Committee.
March	2001	At the request of the Shanghai Animation Film Studio, Kao takes on the character design for *The Heroes of Sui and Tang*. He directs the costuming and coloring for the disciple Kuan-Liang.
July	2001	*JULIET SADNESS* wins the Government Information Office R.O.C., Golden Tripod Awards of Best Comic prize, which is the first girls' manga to win the award in its entire 40+ year history. *Heracles Original Illustrations* is published by Sharp Point Publishing Company Ltd.
October	2001	Together with Mobiking Technologies, Inc., service for downloadable color PHS mobile phone wallpapers, animations, and manga begins.
October	2002	Participates in the 5th Asian Manga Summit and original illustration exhibition held by the Asian Manga Summit Committee.
April	2003	As a joint production with Kuan-Liang, *The Heroes of Sui and Tang 1* is published by Tong Li Publishing Company Ltd. Simplified Chinese edition of *The Heroes of Sui and Tang 1* published by Fecit Publishing Company, Ltd.
September	2003	Simplified Chinese edition of *The Heroes of Sui and Tang 2* published by Fecit Publishing Company, Ltd.

Kuan-Lian

■ Date of Birth: December 27th, 1971
Blood Type: B
Birthplace: Taiwan R.O.C.
Education: Fu Hsing College of Technology,
                Commerce Department of Design

Currently a disciple of the manga artist, Mr. Kao Yung

Serves as trustee for The First Comic Artist Labor Union in Taipei.

Currently a trustee for The Second Comic Artist Labor Union in Taipei

Oversees the Mecha design for Mr. Kao Yung's piece, *Juliet Sadness*.

Creates illustrations to be downloaded together with Mobiking Technologies, Inc., for color PHS mobile phones.

Oversees design, costume, and color work for anime characters in the Shanghai Animation Film Studio production, *The Heroes of Sui and Tang.*

■ **Works**
Grandfather's Weather Forecast /
Hopefully Astrology—the Romance,
a joint production with manga artist Mr. Kao Yung /
What's Happy, a joint production with manga artist Mr. Kao Yung /
First Edition Grimm's Fairy Tales, *Vol. 1—4* with color illustrations /
Short manga series, *Magical Love the Funny Edition /*
The Dusty Racketeers cover illustrations /
The Heroes of Sui and Tang manga /
The Torrent in the World novel series cover illustrations /
Record of Red Dragon Army novel series cover illustrations

October	1999	Serves as trustee for The First Comic Artist Labor Union in Taipei. Participates in the 3rd Asian Manga Summit and original illustration exhibition held by the Asian Manga Summit Committee.
August	2000	Participates in the 4th Asian Manga Summit and original illustration exhibition held by the Asian Manga Summit Committee.
April	2001	At the request of the Shanghai Animation Film Studio, Kuan-Liang oversees the design work for *The Heroes of Sui and Tang* anime characters, and Mr. Kao Yung oversees the design, costume, and color work for the characters.
July	2001	Serves as trustee for The Second Comic Artist Labor Union in Taipei.
October	2002	Participates in the 5th Asian Manga Summit and original illustration exhibition held by the Asian Manga Summit Committee.